378.1
H42   Herman, Simon N.
            American students in
        Israel.

Temple Israel Library
Minneapolis, Minn.

___

Please sign your full name on the above
card.

Return books promptly to the Library or
Temple Office.

Fines will be charged for overdue books
or for damage or loss of same.

DEMCO

AMERICAN STUDENTS IN ISRAEL

AMERICAN STUDENTS IN ISRAEL

Simon N. Herman

Cornell University Press

ITHACA AND LONDON

First published 1970

International Standard Book Number 0-8014-0564-5
Library of Congress Catalog Card Number 77-109338

Printed in the United States of America
by Vail-Ballou Press, Inc.

*To the memory
of my parents*

Acknowledgments

I am grateful to the members of the 1965 American Student Program at the Hebrew University who cheerfully submitted to the many inquisitions of the research. The students who arrived in Israel in subsequent years did not have to suffer for so protracted a period, but their ready cooperation is no less appreciated.

The study began in 1965 and was due to be completed in 1967, a year after the return of the students to the United States. But the years following the study's inception saw such profound changes in both the United States and Israel that by comparison 1965 now appears uneventful and tranquil. While our analysis of the process of cross-cultural education remains essentially unaffected, the altered circumstances could not fail to influence the reactions of students to the sojourn. Accordingly, we extended our study into 1969 to catch the reflections of the changing times and moods.

During a sabbatical year (1968–1969) spent as a Lown research fellow at the Philip W. Lown Graduate Center for Contemporary Jewish Studies of Brandeis University, I was able to renew contact with students who had returned from the sojourn in Israel. I am indebted to Professor Leon Jick, Director of the Graduate Center, for his friendly cooperation, and to Mrs. Betty Starr, Secretary of the Center, for many courtesies.

Acknowledgments

My contacts with students in the United States were also greatly facilitated by Mr. Harold Manson, Director of the Office of Academic Affairs of the American Friends of the Hebrew University; the organization of the follow-up study proceeded smoothly because of the help of Miss Anne Kahn and Mrs. Freda Theaman, both of the Office of Academic Affairs. At the Hebrew University in Jerusalem Dr. Yeheskiel Cohen, Dean of Students, and Mr. Reuven Surkis, formerly Adviser to Overseas Students, extended considerable assistance.

I had the benefit of a critical reading of the first draft of the manuscript by Professor Ben Halpern, of the Lown School of Near Eastern and Judaic Studies at Brandeis University, who gave unstintingly of his advice on the many occasions I consulted him. I also owe much to discussions with Dr. Ozer Schild, of the Department of Psychology at the Hebrew University, who had collaborated with me in an earlier incursion into the field of cross-cultural education.

Mr. David Katz rendered valuable service as research assistant through all stages of the project. Mrs. Nancy Dowty and Mr. Elchanan Gamzu were very helpful in the sections of the study with which they were associated. In the technical preparation of the manuscript I had the competent aid in Jerusalem of Mr. Morris Levy and in Boston of Mrs. Doris Shiffman and Miss Carolyn Cross.

The study was made possible by a research grant from the James Marshall Foundation of New York, supplemented by a grant from the Eliezer Kaplan School of Economics and Social Sciences of the Hebrew University.

SIMON N. HERMAN

Hebrew University of Jerusalem
April 1970

Contents

AMERICAN
STUDENTS
IN ISRAEL

CHAPTER 1

The Foreign Student

Through the centuries students have crossed national boundaries to visit institutions of learning. In recent years the number of student-travelers has risen sharply. Study abroad is no longer the privilege of the few. The "foreign student" and "cross-cultural education" have become subjects of special interest to agencies in the field of international relations, to educational administrators, and more recently to social researchers.[1]

According to a UNESCO survey, at least 350,000 students enrolled for higher education in foreign countries in 1966.[2] Host to by far the largest number of foreign students is the United States, which had more than 82,000 such visitors in 1966, whereas there were only about 36,000 a decade before.[3] While it was serving as host, an estimated 20,000 of its nationals were studying abroad, compared to the approximately 9,500 in 1956.[4]

If we extend the term "student" to those who come to study in other than the regular academic settings, we find that recent years have witnessed a marked diversification in the types of foreign students. Technicians anxious to improve their skills, industrial managers who wish to study better methods of management and production, officials from the governments of new states who need to understand the mechanics of administration, and many others make extended study visits in foreign countries. Thousands of grants—offered by U.N. agencies, by the governments of the respective countries, by universities and educational foundations—are available to aid the student to proceed abroad. The international bodies see in cultural exchanges a means of fostering understanding and cooperation between peoples; the host country not only may wish to provide an educational service, but may hope that the visitors will return to their homes better informed and favorably disposed, and will serve as goodwill emissaries among their own people. Countries have been vying with one another to attract the students, particularly trainees from the many new developing states so sorely in need of skilled manpower.

Complexities of the Cross-Cultural Experience

The educational institutions that serve as hosts now regard it as a matter of considerable practical concern to obtain a proper understanding of the problems of learning and adjustment that confront their foreign visitors. They have begun to recognize the need for a systematic evaluation of the programs of these sojourns with a view to their improvement.[5]

The transition from the total social environment which a country represents to another environment is more complex than is generally supposed. It involves more than the obvious difficulties of mastering a new language, of adapting to a different climate and foods, of understanding foreign customs. A number of the views popularly held about cross-cultural education fail to take into account its intricacies. A case in point is the notion that social contact between students and their hosts leads to better understanding and to improved relations. Yet, many students are known to return to their homeland with a negative feeling about the host country and with hostile attitudes to the former hosts. The mere fact that he is in the country does not mean that the student gets to know his hosts properly. Cultural differences in the method of establishing contact may militate against the meeting of host and guest. The contact when established may be superficial and perfunctory. Even when it gains in depth, what the host seeks to communicate may not always be interpreted correctly, and when understood may not be accepted. Moreover, a better knowledge of the host and his country does not necessarily induce a friendlier attitude.

The popular view at times exaggerates the significance of contact by failing to view it in relation to the student's total experience in the country. Again, generalizations about contact between students and hosts are often based on the fallacious assumption that all sectors of the host society have the same attitude toward the visitors. The student may have occasion to meet one sector and not another.

Research has been giving attention to the part played by social contact in intergroup relations within a given culture.[6] Although the findings are still largely inconclusive, the research has led to a clearer formulation of the significant questions and could be used as a starting point for an attack on a wide range of unexplored problems connected with the establishment and development of social contact between students socialized in a particular culture and their foreign hosts. What conditions facilitate the establishment of the contact, and what kind of contact is likely to produce what kind of results?[7]

Further questions arise. In recent years, with the growing

number of organized exchange programs, students have increasingly arrived in groups. How does the adjustment of the student who lives alone in the foreign country as an isolated individual differ from that of students who are part of a group? Is the clustering together of students from a particular country a desirable phenomenon? In any event, the function of the group of fellow-strangers needs to be analyzed. And there are other groups to be reckoned with. How much is the student still influenced by groups from home; on what questions and in what circumstances does he turn to groups in his new surroundings as sources of reference?

Little is known about the optimal duration for a study visit; this will obviously depend upon its purpose. A visit should conceivably be long enough to permit the desired amount of learning and also to allow for a measure of adjustment to the host country without resulting in the estrangement or alienation of the student from the home country to which he is expected to return. The development of such general criteria for the determination of optimal duration presupposes an analysis of the processes of learning and of adjustment in the new culture.

The foreign student, socialized in his native culture, is called upon to learn, and often act in accordance with, the different norms of the new culture. Under what conditions and on what subjects does he accept the communications of his hosts? What are the implications of allowing the student to become a participant in certain fields of activity rather than remain just a passive learner?

The analysis of the *process* of change as it unfolds in the cross-cultural situation has received scant attention. To what extent are the changes on the perceptual, on the value, or on the action levels? Some studies indicate that the changes are mainly in perception, but how and why this is so needs fuller examination. The changes to be observed relate not only to the country of sojourn but also to the perception of the home country. And the further question arises—to what extent and in what circumstances do the changes persist when the student returns to his home?

Apart from the importance of research on these and other questions for the proper development of cross-cultural education, it becomes clear that the cross-cultural situation provides a strategic vantage point for the study of a number of processes of general interest to the social scientist. In recent years there has accordingly been increasing research in this area, more particularly on foreign students in the United States. The main published studies relate to Swedish, Mexican, German, Japanese, Indian and Scandinavian students in the United States. There has been comparatively little research on foreign students in other countries.[8] Several studies have dealt with Americans abroad.[9]

The Special Position of the American Jewish Students in Israel

The present study of Americans abroad has an added dimension. These were Jewish students with a special position in the structure of the home society as members of a minority group and, at the same time, with a peculiar involvement as Jews in the host country of Israel.

For many foreign students one issue, or set of issues, may deeply affect the experience of their sojourn.[10] Thus, the problems of the Japanese overseas student have been described in terms of a search for identity.[11] Again, students —especially from young, developing countries—are often sensitive to questions of national status; a discrepancy between a student's conception of his country's status and his hosts' conception of it may color his entire attitude to the country of sojourn and its people, particularly when the self-esteem of the student is linked up with the question of national status.[12]

The reactions of the American Jewish students who come to Israel are likely to be influenced by a unique cluster of issues. They come to Israel with a prior emotional attachment to it which is not usually found among students sojourning in a foreign land. Because of the historical relationship which exists between Israel and Jews everywhere, they do not see the country as foreign nor themselves as foreigners. They expect to feel "at home" in what by many Jews is considered a Jewish homeland. They hope that the Jewishness which set them off from others in the United States will serve as the bond between themselves and their Israeli hosts, that it will provide them with an entrance card into what is there a majority group. Their feeling about the sojourn will conceivably be affected by the extent to which these hopes for the encounter with Israel and with Israelis are fulfilled.

The American Jewish students differ in yet another respect from other foreign students. The expectations are that a student visiting a foreign country will return home after the completion of his studies; he may give little or no thought to settlement in the country of sojourn, and the hosts generally look upon him as just a foreign sojourner. Not all students resist the temptation to remain because of the superior career opportunities an advanced host country may offer them. Greatest magnet of all has been the United States, and on the conclusion of their studies many students from abroad have elected to throw in their lot with their hosts, to the dismay of their former homelands which are thus deprived of the talents and training of promising sons and daughters.[13] On the other hand, it is rare for American students studying abroad to settle in a less advantaged country. In the case with which we are concerned, however, American students, because of their relationship as Jews to Israel and in response to a variety of social pressures, invariably begin to consider—if they have not already done so before their coming—their willingness to settle in the host country.

The Need for a Conceptual Framework

The published studies are for the most part reports of empirical findings and do not adequately explore the process involved in the cross-cultural experience. Reviews of these studies have recognized the need for a more theoretical consideration. Further advances in the study of cross-cultural education will depend upon placing it more clearly within a conceptual framework linking up with broader theory.

We shall suggest a series of conceptual contexts for the analysis of cross-cultural education and will then proceed to view the reactions of our subjects within this framework. Although we shall seek to map out the common ground between our enquiry and others in the field, our main concern will be the peculiarly Jewish facets. At the same time this dimension of difference may help clarify some aspects of the general process in the cross-cultural experience.

The student in the cross-cultural situation, poised between two cultures, by each of which he is influenced in greater or lesser measure, is an eminently suitable subject for the examination of multiple group references. Our students, as members of a minority subculture in the American majority culture and as persons sharing a common group

7

belongingness as Jews with the Israeli hosts, bring the issue of multiple group references into unusually sharp focus.

The influence of prior emotional involvement in the host country has not been considered in the studies of cross-cultural education. In our study the degree of involvement is unusually high and its influence is accordingly much more patent.

CHAPTER 2

The Psychological Field
of the Foreign Student

Cross-cultural education is a particular instance of re-education. We may define it as a process of change—in cognition, in feelings, and in action—occurring in individuals socialized in one culture, as a result of their sojourn for educational purposes in a different culture.

The definition suggests a number of foci for the analysis of the psychological field of the foreign student. We may view the student visiting a foreign country as (1) a person in a new psychological situation; (2) a stranger on the periphery of the host society; (3) a person in overlapping situations, i.e., subject simultaneously to influences from groups in the home and host country; and (4) a person with a specific time perspective. Such analysis may permit a systematic approach to the multiplicity of issues which, as we noted in the previous chapter, arise in a study of the cross-cultural experience. We may also hope to derive hypotheses about the determinants of change in this situation.[1]

A New Psychological Situation

The fact that the host-culture is "different" means that the student enters a situation which is new to him. The "cognitive maps" which he learned in his home culture are no longer trustworthy guides; he undergoes what has been termed a "culture shock." An immigrant who has just now arrived is, of course, in a similar position. The student's sojourn, however, is limited in time. While for the immigrant the period of transition is brief compared to his total stay in his adopted country, for the student this period occupies a relatively prominent place. As a result, the student's behavior even at a late stage of his visit may be influenced by his initial experiences.

Two questions are of special interest in this context. What characterizes the process of perception of the new situation? What are the effects of the new situation on the student's behavior?

Differentiation and organization. A new situation is characterized by a lack of differentiation. The regions which constitute the psychological environment are few and large, and there is no clear demarcation of boundaries. Consequently, satisfaction or frustration about a given event often is not localized but infiltrates into other regions as well. This explains in part the sweeping generalizations of the tourist describing the impressions of a fleeting visit. Even when with the passage of time a certain measure of differentiation sets in, boundaries between regions are not always firm and there is a continued spreading of satisfaction or dissatisfaction about one aspect of the country's life to another.

Evidence of such effect is provided in a cross-cultural study by Lysgaard.[2] In interviews with Norwegian Fulbright grantees who had returned from a sojourn in the United States he found that in each of two broad areas satisfaction was "generalized" from one item to another. Lysgaard indicates that the generalization does not reflect any personality trait of the subjects but seems to be due to "characteristics of the person in the situation." We would interpolate "new situation" and would submit that Lysgaard's findings could well be analyzed in terms of the relative lack of differentiation and the consequent "spreading" of impressions.

The differentiation which increases with time may be followed by a reorganization of the impressions around a few key elements that will eventually determine the organization of the experience as a whole. Thus, in assessing the outcomes of the sojourn, it may not be essential to study the entire welter of impressions experienced by the students; it is important rather to pinpoint those dominant items which have determined the final pattern of impressions.

This process of organization, however, may be delayed by the tension frequently accompanying the experience of the student in his new environment. There may be an extended initial period in which the student receives new percepts without organizing them, and then after a while (and this may conceivably be only after the return home) a rapid organization of the percepts may take place.

The stranger group. The essence of a new psychological situation is that, in addition to being undifferentiated, it is unstructured. Being in such an unstructured situation is tantamount to being on soft, unstable ground. The person is not clearly aware of the potentialities in the situation, of the paths by which a goal can be reached, and of the possible outcomes of an intended action. The immediate psychological result is enhanced insecurity, and in such circumstances the individual will often seek the security which acceptance into a group can give. In addition, the fact of being in an unknown situation increases the dependence on the "social reality" provided by a group. Although the need for verifying vague hunches and ambiguous communications about the nature of the environment is strong, several ways of verification which under ordinary circumstances could be utilized are now closed. The person in this new situation has not the background knowledge against which to test impressions; furthermore, the credibility of the source of a given communication is often as much in doubt as is the communication itself. Thus the stranger is forced to rely on other ways of verification, among these group verification.

This phenomenon of increased group-attractiveness, which appears to be of general validity for a person in a new situation, assumes special importance for the stranger in a foreign society. The home groups with which he previously has been in face-to-face contact are now separated from him by sheer geographical distance, and cannot fulfil for him all of the functions which they had previously discharged. They can no longer serve as his "social ground" in the foreign country nor would they be competent to verify information and opinions, even if such verifications were technically feasible, on the problems which now are the most salient for him. And since these needs are particularly high in the new environment, the stranger will be strongly attracted to a group which can meet them.

The group most readily available to satisfy these requirements is composed of strangers in the same position—the "stranger-group." Schachter has shown that the affiliative motive aroused by anxiety is directed toward persons in the same situation.[3] It can thus be expected that a stranger's insecurity will make him turn to other strangers with a similar background which qualifies them in his eyes to become credible providers of social reality for him. In this way, an interdependence is established: each stranger obtains security and verification from the others who in their turn are equally dependent on him.

We can accordingly predict that, when a number of strangers together face a foreign society, a strongly cohesive association will be formed. Its members will influence each other's perceptions of the foreign environment and attitudes toward it. Of considerable importance in any study of cross-cultural education are (1) the presence or absence of fellow-strangers to whom the newcomer can refer, and (2) the norms, favorable or unfavorable to the host-country, developed in such a group.

A Stranger in the Host Society

The student in a foreign country is in the position of a "stranger." [4] From his location on the periphery of the host society, its norms and role-performances are less visible to him than they are to its members, and he is not clearly aware of the range of permissible deviations.[5] Moreover, the codes which regulated his conduct in the home culture do not always apply, and the deeply ingrained tendency to act in accordance with them may at times make him oblivious of the fact that other norms prevail or may render difficult the adoption of the behavior required by the host society.

The student-stranger is usually eager to shed his strangeness and become acquainted with members of the host society. Different cultures, however, have different ways of establishing contact, and this fact may be a barrier to interaction between strangers and hosts. Kurt Lewin, in his analysis of the social psychological differences between the United States and Germany, has stated:

The average social distance between different individuals seems to be smaller in the United States so far as the surface regions, or as one may say, the "peripheral regions" of the personality are concerned. That means the American is more willing to be open to other individuals and to share certain situations with other individuals than the German. . . . The American seems more friendly and more ready to help a stranger.[6]

The position of a foreign student in the United States, where contact is speedily established, may be easier than that of the American in a number of foreign countries where the culturally-constrained reserve of the hosts disappoints his expectations of quick acquaintanceship. On the other hand, the foreign student in the United States is often at a loss to understand why the first, quick contact, with the expectations of friendship it arouses, does not readily progress beyond the "peripheral regions."

When the contact is established, the stranger's learning in the new environment depends on the extent to which the host provides direct information on the norms of the host society or cues that allow for inference. This will in turn depend on the host's attitude to the stranger and may differ greatly from sector to sector in the society.

A given sector of the host society may actively desire, passively agree, or be unwilling to accept the stranger. Three types of groups may then be distinguished: the "open," which not only agrees to accept the stranger but itself initiates contact and encourages his integration; the "indifferent," which is prepared to accept him if he takes the initiative but leaves it to him to overcome any barriers; the "closed," which is disinclined to accept him. It remains to explore the differences in the learning and adjustment of the stranger in each of these three sectors.

The circumstances under which the communications of the hosts are accepted also merit fuller exploration than they have had in studies of cross-cultural education. We suggest that the probability of acceptance will be highest when the communicator is perceived as similar in background to the stranger and as disinterested, i.e., having no desire to convert the stranger, and when the stranger feels himself under no compulsion to accept the communication.

The sojourn of the stranger is crowded with impressions of the host society whose operations are new to him at a multiplicity of points, and only a limited segment of his new experiences involve direct interaction with the hosts. Even within this segment there are likely to be limitations to what and from whom he is prepared to learn. Thus another form of learning, "by observation," may assume considerable importance, possibly greater than the explicit messages or the cues provided in the course of interaction with the hosts. By his observations of the host society the stranger learns what are the actual norms and permitted deviations, rather than the formal, declared ideology.

A further characteristic of student-strangers is their position as recipients. Although the student may actively seek out experiences, he is still a listener and receiver rather than a doer and giver. Frequently this role is accompanied by a marked contraction of the student's life-space, as compared with the range of his activities in his home country. In this position of relative passivity and dependence, and at times of a status lower than that accorded to him at home, tensions are engendered which may impair the learning process. On the other hand, if the student can become an active participant or helper in the host-country, the conditions for effective learning and adjustment improve. He is then in fact taking a decided step forward into the host society and away from his position on the periphery as stranger.

Overlapping Situations

The foreign student may be seen as a person in a series of overlapping situations—he is located within the common part of two or more psychological situations which exist simultaneously for him. Unlike the tourist, the student is compelled to reach a *modus vivendi* with the host society for the duration of his stay. On the other hand, unlike the immigrant, the student comtemplates a return to the home culture. He is more likely than either tourist or immigrant to find himself in overlapping situations. While maintaining his ties with the home culture, he cannot, and often does not wish to, ignore the demands of the host culture in which he is a sojourner. When the norms differ the question arises which of the competing groups has the greater potency, i.e., determines the student's attitudes and behavior.

In a study of multiple-group membership, Killian has analyzed the dilemma of the individual who has to choose between the demands of competing groups when catastrophe strikes a community.[7] The choice is generally determined by family loyalty, but some factors dispose the individual to adhere to secondary-group demands even in a disaster. Killian points to the need for further research to make possible the prediction of the choice an individual will make in such situations of role-conflict.

In their experiment on cross-cultural norm conflict, French and Zajonc [8] raise two hypotheses: (1) that behavior in a situation involving pressures to conformity to two different normative ideals occurs at the intersection of the two corresponding force-fields, and (2) that when potency of membership is manipulated, the point of intersection between the two norms and thus the resulting behavior is shifted in the direction of the normative ideal of the group whose potency is increased and away from the ideal of the group whose potency is decreased. This experiment does not, however, investigate the determinants of potency.

Barker [9] suggests that "potency" and "valence" together

determine behavior in overlapping situations. Potency is de-fined as "the influence of one situation relative to all simul-taneously acting situations" and valence as "the characteris-tics of objects and behavior possibilities that cause a person to approach or withdraw from them; on a conscious level this is experienced as attractiveness (positive valence) and repulsiveness (negative valence)."

Modifying somewhat the definition of potency given by Barker, we define it as the *effect* that a situation has on be-havior, and we then regard valence as *one of the determi-nants* of potency. We submit that the other determinant is salience, in the sense of relative prominence in the cognitive field, the "figure" against the "ground." [10]

Several experimental studies have been conducted on the salience of groups.[11] After heightening the subjects' aware-ness of their membership in a specific group by vivid re-minders, the experimenters investigated the effect of the group's increased salience in the given situation in produc-ing change or resistance to change. Thus, in one of the ex-periments the reminder to the students gathered in a room when a questionnaire was administered that they were Catholics resulted in more answers conforming to Catholic norms than were given by students in another room who received no such reminder. Presumably, the valence of Ca-tholicism was equal for the students in the two rooms, but its heightened salience increased its potency for those in the first room and determined the nature of their responses.[12]

Students arriving in a foreign country become more aware of their own nationality, which sets them off from their hosts—their nationality by this juxtaposition becomes more salient. Whether or not their regard for their own na-tionality grows may depend upon other considerations. Its valence may be influenced by the esteem in which the hosts—to the extent that the hosts are accepted as a normative reference group—hold the nationality of the foreign students; it may be affected by the comparison, favorable or unfavorable, that the student makes between his own country and the country of sojourn, between his own people and his hosts. It would seem to us that the study of cross-cultural education must concern itself with the changing salience, as well as the valence, of reference groups in the home and host countries.[13]

Changes which run counter to the norms of the home culture can presumably be effected more easily when the salience of those norms is low.[14] The question is whether changes effected under such circumstances will be maintained when the students return home. The changes may have a better chance of survival if attention is drawn to the home norms during the influence process; when the students return they are already equipped to cope with the criticism their deviation arouses.

Time Perspective

The orientation of the student to his sojourn, implied in our definition of cross-cultural education by the phrase "for educational purposes," influences the entire course of the cross-cultural process. It would conceivably have been more accurate to have said: "for ostensibly educational purposes," because the avowed educational intent does not always exhaust the motivational content of the student's approach to his sojourn. Other considerations may weigh more importantly with him than the academic aims. Just as some students come primarily to study their specific disciplines, so others may come primarily to learn about the country and its people.

Whatever the student's goals, the period for their attainment is always limited. The awareness of the transient nature of his stay and the prospect of an earlier or later return to his permanent home may determine in no small measure his reactions to his hosts and their country.

The influence of a given time perspective on the cross-cultural experience can be understood properly only if time perspective is analyzed in terms of its various dimensions. The dimensions relevant to our present subject would seem to be the following: past-present-future orientation, scope, structure and differentiation.[15]

Past-present-future orientation. Both past and future as perceived by the individual constitute part of his psychological field, influencing his present perception and behavior. Conversely, present needs and values influence the perception of the past and future. The orientation of a given individual in a particular situation may be primarily to the past, the present, or the future. Optimal functioning is generally facilitated by a balance among the three.[16] When the orientation is to the future, importance attaches to the controllability of locomotion, i.e., to the felt chance of reaching goals set for the future.

Scope refers to the range of the time perspective, i.e., how far into the past or into the future it extends. The scope may be narrow, limited to events which occurred only a short while ago or which are immediately impending; or it may be broad, stretching extensively into a more distant past or forward into a more distant future.

Structure concerns the organization of the time perspective. While the scope of the time perspective of an individual in relation to a given situation may be broad—he may see far into the past or into the future—his time perspective may yet be unstructured, he may have only the vaguest notion of the paths by which the distant goal may be reached;

or, again, it may be clearly structured, he may foresee the precise steps that have to be taken.

Differentiation denotes the division of the time perspective into a series of time sequences. The degree of differentiation, or what is sometimes termed the density of the time perspective,[17] is defined by the number of such distinguishable sequences.

The relationship between time perspective and other variables may now be examined in terms of the dimensions we have delineated. Thus, wide scope is productive of involvement and long-term planning, both of which tend to produce consistency in behavior over time. In an experiment carried out by Barker, Dembo, and Lewin,[18] children showed greater constructiveness in long play units than in shorter ones.

Wide scope of time perspective reduces the importance of contemporaneous stimuli and hence diminishes the probability of change. On the other hand, if change is in fact attained under conditions of wide scope of time perspective, it is likely to be more enduring. Conversely, susceptibility to change is highest when the scope of time perspective is restricted; at the same time, the permanence of such change is doubtful.

Structurization, assuming that a measure of controllability of locomotion exists, is a prerequisite for morale.[19] Wide scope with a low degree of structurization leads to anxiety and low morale. Where the future is broken up into a series of time sequences each with a subgoal, i.e., where there is differentiation, anxiety may be allayed and morale raised by the achievements within each time sequence and the possibility of preparing for the next sequence.

When students arrive in the host country, the scope of

their future time perspective is limited to the arrangements immediately ahead. The degree of structurization is usually low and so is the degree of differentiation. While the past is still relatively prominent, the demands of the present become increasingly pressing. This situation is likely to produce a susceptibility to expedient behavior changes but a low susceptibility to permanent changes. After the initial elation has worn off, the absence of structurization and differentiation may bring about a lowering of morale. As the sojourn progresses, past time perspective often becomes less salient and there is accordingly a greater readiness for lasting changes. The measure of structurization and differentiation increases and as a result morale improves. Toward the end of the sojourn, the "back home" situation becomes salient. If what lies ahead in that situation is unstructured a pervasive anxiety may set in.

We have referred to time perspective in terms of the time dimension in the student's view of his sojourn. We turn now to two other usages of time perspective which may be relevant.

One usage relates to the time orientation characteristic of a stage in development—we shall call it the "developmental stage of time perspective." The life-space of the infant does not extend beyond the immediate present; gradually as part of the process of growth, a sense of time perspective develops, and a rapid extension of scope—with but little structuring—occurs in adolescence. Many students are in precisely this stage of development, a period during which they are in search of answers to the questions about the future. For some of them too the sojourn abroad may allow for what Erikson has termed a "psychological moratorium," [20] a stalling period between adolescence and adulthood.

Time perspective may also refer to the temporal context in which a phenomenon (in this case, a country) is perceived. It is what we would term "historical time perspective"—the evaluation of the country's present in relation to its past and to its plans or aspirations. A student who views the country within the context of its strivings in the past and its goals for the future is likely to have a deeper, often different, understanding of what he perceives than his fellow-student who sees the country only as it is at the moment in which he visits it.

CHAPTER 3

Background and
Method of Study

Israel has a special interest in attracting Jewish students to its universities. Regarding itself as the center of Jewish life, it feels called upon to provide an educational service designed to enrich the Jewish background and strengthen the sense of Jewish identity of the students who sojourn within its borders. Moreover, it views the students as a link between Israel and the Diaspora; it also hopes that some of them as a result of the sojourn will decide to throw in their lot with Israel and settle there permanently. Since the Six Day War of June 1967, this last objective has gained greatly in emphasis.

Israel as a Study Center

Jewish students have been coming to Israel from all parts of the globe, from all countries which allow them to proceed for study abroad. More than 5,000 such students were in Israel at the beginning of the 1969–1970 academic year —at the Hebrew University of Jerusalem and at its Haifa College, at the University of Tel Aviv, at Bar-Ilan University in Ramat Gan, at the Haifa Technion, at the Weizmann Institute of Science in Rehovot, and at the newly arising University of the Negev in Beersheba.

While all these universities play a part in the reception of the students, the leading role has been taken by the Hebrew University, which sees itself as a veritable "university of the Jewish people." Apart from accepting students into its regular courses, it has initiated several special programs for them, the chief of which is the American Student Program (A.S.P.), recently renamed the One Year Program, organized by the American Friends of the Hebrew University. There were 175 students from abroad enrolled at the Hebrew University at the beginning of the present decade (in the 1959–1960 academic year); by the 1969–1970 academic year the number had grown to 3,200, drawn from 51 countries, and constituting as much as 20 per cent of the University's student body.

Students also come in groups under the direct auspices of their home universities. One American university—Brandeis—annually provides facilities for its students to spend five months of study in Jerusalem, and several other American universities have entered into cooperative arrangements with the Israeli institutions whereby their students may pursue part of their studies in Israel.

It has long been customary for young Orthodox Jews to come to the *yeshivot* (religious academies) of Israel; in addition, in recent years the Jewish Theological Seminary of America (Conservative) and the Hebrew Union College-Jewish Institute of Religion (Reform) have established branches in Jerusalem to which their students come for a year of their curriculum of studies toward the rabbinate. The seminaries for Jewish teachers in several countries similarly require their students to take a part of their training in Israel. Special programs for them have been provided by the Greenberg and the Gold Institutes of the Jewish Agency, and training at a university level has recently been made available at the Hebrew University's Center for Jewish Education in the Diaspora. The World Zionist Organization has for the past twenty-one years maintained an institute providing one-year courses for the training of youth leaders from abroad in which over 3,800 students from thirty-seven countries have participated.

Indeed a period of study in Israel is increasingly recognized as an important complement to the training of personnel engaged in Jewish professional service. If we go beyond the term "student" in its stricter sense, we find that a considerable number of veteran workers in the Jewish field —in particular teachers of Hebrew and of Jewish subjects —come to Israel for refresher courses. A seminar for world Jewish service, designed for key executives of Jewish organizations, has been initiated by the Hebrew University's Institute of Contemporary Jewry, and in time this seminar may be expanded into a comprehensive Jewish "civil service" training program.

Many Jewish educators now hold that not only a training for professional service but also the Jewish education of the layman is incomplete without, at least, a study visit to Israel. A variety of frameworks exists for such visits; summer institutes alone draw several thousand students each year. There are also students who participate in work projects such as the *sherut la'am* (service to the people) and *sh'nat sherut* (year of service).

Although Israel mainly attracts Jewish students, it also serves as a study center for Christian scholars who come for seminars in the "land of the Bible." Israel in addition welcomes—at the Afro-Asian Institute of the Histadruth (General Federation of Labor) and at other institutions— trainees from the developing states who wish to learn about certain aspects of its development. Special university facilities for training in medicine and other fields have been provided for students from these countries.

The American Student Program

We studied a succession of groups of American Jewish students visiting Israel. Our principal focus in the present study is on a group that came to the Hebrew University for the 1965–1966 academic year. A preliminary analysis of the data obtained from them indicated the desirability of securing further material; accordingly we carried out a supplementary study on the largely similar group that arrived under the same program for the 1966–1967 academic year. These students were in Israel during the Six Day War and we were able to observe their reactions to the events of that period.

In the summer of 1965, eighty-seven American students reached Israel for a year at the Hebrew University under the American Student Program. During the first three months of their sojourn they studied—along with other students from abroad—at an *ulpan* (a seminar for the intensive study of Hebrew). With the opening of the Hebrew University's academic year in November they entered on the regular courses in their fields of interest. Five students left before the end of the academic year (for personal reasons unconnected with the sojourn in Israel); the rest remained until its conclusion and returned to the United States after the examinations in July and August.

Fifty-nine of the students were entering their junior year at college; [1] the remainder were at a more advanced stage in their studies. There were twice as many women (fifty-nine) as men (twenty-eight) in the group. Nine of the students had immigrated as young children with their parents to the United States, twenty-three were second generation Americans, and fifty-five, third generation. Included among them were members of Orthodox, Conservative, and Reform congregations, as well as students who declared themselves to be nonreligious.[2] The formal Jewish education they had received—from Jewish day schools to Sunday school classes—differed in extent and in depth. Noteworthy was the large number who had attended Jewish summer camps; students from the Conservative movement were particularly emphatic about the contribution their attendance at the Ramah camps had made to their interest in Israel.

The fact that these students had chosen to come to Israel and were favorably disposed to it in itself indicates that they occupied certain ideological positions in American Jewish life. The variations of attitude on Jewish issues were not as wide nor as distinct as they would be in a representative sample of Jewish students in the United States. The main concern of our study is with the reactions to the sojourn characteristic of the group as a whole, although we also refer to the differences in viewpoint that prevailed on a number of issues. This is essentially a case study in which the group of visiting students is *ab initio* favorably disposed toward, and deeply involved in, the host country.

The Research Instruments

A study in cross-cultural education should properly start before the sojourn begins and should include one or more enquiries during the sojourn, an enquiry at its termination, and a follow-up at one or two points after the return to the home country. In the present research it was found possible to begin the study of the entire group of students on board the ship bound for Israel, to maintain close contact with them throughout the period of their year-long sojourn in Israel, and to restudy them a year after their return to the United States.[3]

In our analysis we combine quantitative and qualitative data obtained from a variety of sources—questionnaires, interviews with individuals and with groups, diaries, essays, letters, and observation.

The questionnaires. The first questionnaire was administered on board ship in mid-July 1965.[4] It provided the base line for the changes to be studied. Toward the end of February 1966, a second questionnaire was administered. It contained a number of the questions which had appeared in the first and enabled us to determine the changes which had occurred in the interval.

A third questionnaire, mailed to the students a year after their return, repeated some of the questions of the second and included others relating specifically to the experiences of the year back in the States. This questionnaire reached the students during the first days of June on the eve of the Six Day War. Their reactions were undoubtedly colored by the events of the period (some expressly state this), and in assessing their answers to several of the questions it is accordingly difficult to disentangle the effects of the year back in the United States from the changes produced by the impact of the war. Some indication of the influence of the year back in the United States may, however, be gleaned from the responses of the students to open-end questions.

Thirty-six students (41 per cent) returned completed questionnaires from the United States.[5] Of these, twenty-nine had completed the second questionnaire in Israel; their responses on the two were compared.

The Semantic Differential. In the final section of the questionnaire we sought through the use of a semantic-differential rating instrument (developed by Osgood and his associates) [6] to ascertain how the students perceived and evaluated the following concepts: "American Jew," "American non-Jew," "Israeli," "myself as I am," and "myself as I would like to be." The students were requested to rate each concept on identical lists of twenty-one bipolar adjective scales (such as "industrious–lazy," "courteous––discourteous," "sociable–unsociable"). Each set of adjectives was ranged along a seven-point scale.

All five concepts appeared in the first questionnaire; in the second we limited ourselves (in order not to impose unduly on the patience of the students) to three: "American Jew," "Israeli," and "myself as I am."

The panel group. Ten students randomly selected constituted a panel group, and were subjected individually to intensive, focused interviews at the beginning, toward the middle, and at the end of their sojourn. In addition the interviewees were invited to two group sessions where a number of key questions were presented to them for discussion. Every effort was made to ensure an easy, informal atmosphere for these sessions, and the students responded eagerly. Several members of the panel later on their return to the United States wrote letters to the author describing their first reactions to their old surroundings.

Individual interviews. Interviews were carried out on three occasions during the sojourn. On the day of their arrival and again a month later the students were approached informally, as they were walking on the campus or sitting in the cafeteria, in order to obtain their current impressions of Israel. The third interview, on the eve of their departure for the United States, took place in their rooms and was more intensive. Every second student (randomly selected) was interviewed on this occasion.

Diaries and essays. In response to a request, accompanied by a promise that personal references would be regarded as confidential, several students handed the author of this study the diaries they had kept during the sojourn. The students had kept the diaries without any thought that such a request would be made.

A number of the overseas students at the Hebrew University participated in the lecture courses in social psychology given by the author, and as one of their assignments wrote essays reviewing their experiences in Israel. Among the essays were fifty-four written by American students.

Observation. Members of the research team had occasion to observe the students in a number of settings, particularly on the occasion of their *tiyulim* (excursions into the country). The *madrichim* (counselors) attached to the students also reported to the research team on their observations.

Supplementary sources. A questionnaire designed to fill in gaps in the material obtained from the 1965–1966 group was administered in November 1966 at a gathering of the 1966–1967 American Student Program participants at which eighty-three students were present.

After the Six Day War a brief questionnaire was prepared in order to gauge the impact of the events on the students. The questionnaire was left in the offices of the adviser to overseas students and was completed by the thirty-three members of the A.S.P. who happened to call at the offices for a variety of administrative arrangements before their departure in July and August. There is no reason to believe that any selective factor of significance operated to make their responses unrepresentative of the group.

Toward the end of 1968 the author spent part of his sabbatical year at Brandeis University in the United States; he took occasion to meet many of the students in the New England and New York areas who had returned from the sojourn in Israel and discuss with them their experiences after returning to the States. In addition, a questionnaire containing a few open-end questions about these experiences was circulated among students who had been in the American Student Program since 1965. Seventy-eight students replied, i.e., just over 20 per cent of those who had been in Israel during the years 1965–1968.[7]

During 1965—and also in earlier years—we had occasion to administer questionnaires to, and conduct interviews with, students at the Institute for Youth Leaders from Abroad conducted by the Youth Department of the World Zionist Organization in Jerusalem. An opportunity had also arisen to interview students of the Institute after their return to the United States. The program of the Institute differs in important respects from that of the A.S.P. at the Hebrew University; besides the months in Jerusalem, students of the Institute spend periods at work in kibbutzim and in immigrant settlements. A number of these students are leaders of Zionist youth organizations and are more likely to form an intention to settle. We shall make occasional reference to the material obtained from students of the Institute on points on which the material from the A.S.P. students is not sufficiently comprehensive—specifically, on problems of social contact in the kibbutzim and on the process leading to a decision to settle in Israel.

A number of students who had been members of the A.S.P. and the Institute of earlier years had either remained for further studies or had returned to settle in Israel. One of them supplied us with a detailed diary he had kept. In the course of interviews with twelve student-settlers, questions were asked about their experiences as settlers. In addition two group interviews were held in 1969 with members of the A.S.P. who had returned to settle, one interview with five and the other with four students.

Relationship with research team. The students were highly cooperative and some of those not selected for interviewing expressed disappointment at their omission. The students indeed saw in the research team a group of persons who sought to understand them, not to "propagandize" or influence them. Several stated that the discussions with the research team allowed a much needed opportunity for a full and free ventilation of the problems which agitated them.

The two main interviewers were university graduates in the social sciences from English-speaking countries who had settled in Israel—the one a South African pursuing graduate studies in the department of sociology and the other an American housewife. The students seemed to extend them both their full confidence and spoke frankly.

CHAPTER 4

Israeli Hosts and Their Student Guests: Communalities and Differences

Students who come to the United States generally do so because of the opportunities for specialized training which its advanced educational institutions provide. American students proceeding abroad may have less specific academic objectives in mind; they nonetheless tend to see the sojourn in a foreign culture in the first instance as a learning experience related to the education they are acquiring.

For the Jewish students who came to Israel the academic side of their stay was of secondary import; they came because of their interest in a country to which they saw themselves related by virtue of their Jewishness. Among the students were some who were thinking of a career in the Rabbinate or in the field of Jewish education, and who were thus specifically interested in the Jewish studies at the University or in improving their proficiency in Hebrew. But they too were primarily interested in the country. When asked their principal reason for choosing Israel rather than some other country, the great majority of the students gave reasons linking Israel with the Jewish people, its history, and culture.

Even when the students have intensely personal reasons for the decision to proceed abroad, it is their link with the country as Jews which determines the choice of Israel as

33

the location of the sojourn. Thus, a student begins by list-
ing the more personal factors: "I wanted to escape the pressures of a steady boy friend whom I did not want to
marry, I wanted to get away from the pampering of a
mother whom I did not get along with." But then she observes: "These problems could have been resolved anywhere. Why did I choose Israel? I have gone to Yeshiva
for twelve years, and my entire Jewish background has
been such as to make me love Israel and want to come to
it."

In the interviews students frequently reiterated that for
them Israel was in a separate category from other potentially interesting and stimulating countries.

I came here because of my connection with Judaism. Not because of any other connection. Otherwise I wouldn't be interested in Israel.

To begin with I'm a Jew, and a Jew who has received a Jewish education. Naturally I've always had an intense desire to
visit Israel, the birth-place and home of my people.

All of us, I think, came to Israel secretly hoping to find something special for ourselves, a place with which we could identify and where we could feel at home, although outwardly
our purpose for being in Israel was to continue our university
education in a somewhat different and thus more broadening
setting.

While Israel was foremost in my mind, I did for a time consider studying elsewhere, in France or England for example.
. . . I felt an attraction to Israel because it is a Jewish State
and therefore a place where I felt that I could comfortably
belong, while in any other country I would be a stranger—
an American and a Jew, doubly separated from the people.

The students expect that the Jewishness which they share with their hosts will be a bridge to mutual understanding and social acceptance. There may, however, be unanticipated differences about this very Jewishness which they had hitherto perceived as the common denominator between themselves and their hosts.

Variations in the Common Identity

Although they live in so many diverse environments, Jews have maintained everywhere a kernel of sameness that can be designated as peculiarly "Jewish." At the same time their socialization in the different cultures has produced variations in the common identity. The differences are likely to be particularly pronounced when one environment is that in which Jews are a minority while in the other they constitute the majority. Moreover, a Jewish identity (or, more correctly, subidentity) exists nowhere in isolation; it is in every country joined in interaction with another ethnic [1] subidentity the influence of which is imprinted on it.

What then are the common elements and differences that influence the nature of the meeting between the hosts as Israeli Jews and their guests as American Jews? To find the answer, we must examine the relationship between the American and Jewish subidentities which constitute the ethnic identity of the American Jewish student as compared with the relationship between the Israeli and Jewish subidentities of the Israeli host. Pertinent to such an analysis are the degree of overlap between the subidentities, the measure of their consonance, with whom they align and from whom they mark off, and their relative strength or potency. From this examination it may become clearer how "being Jewish" expresses itself in the American and

Israel environments, what expectations about the Jewishness of their hosts the American Jewish students are likely to bring with them, and at what points the reality will differ from these expectations.

The American Jew tends to see his Jewishness as relevant only in certain settings and on certain occasions—his being Jewish is related to specific, limited regions of the life space. There is a sharp demarcation between specifically Jewish and general activities. As a student put it: "In the States there are definite times—such as on the Chagim [festivals]—when you behave as a Jew. The society around you is behaving in a different way." The majority of the students in our study saw no connection between "feeling Jewish" and "feeling American" (Tables 1 and 2).

While the amount of overlap between Americanism and Jewishness is small, "being Jewish" and "being Israeli" are seen as pertaining in common to a large number of regions. A study of a representative sample of an Israeli high school population (eleventh graders) found that only a small minority failed to observe a connection between the two subidentities [2] (Tables 3 and 4).

Insofar as lines of demarcation can be observed between the subidentities, they are clearer to overseas-born than to native Israelis since the former acquired the Israeli subidentity after the Jewish. Again, for religious Israelis there are clearly defined regions of religious observance which are seen as pertaining to the Jewish subidentity only, but in other regions they will often not clearly distinguish between what is Israeli and what is Jewish. As for native nonreligious Israelis, they have difficulty in indicating how their "being Jewish" specifically expresses itself. The visiting students on their part may have difficulty in discovering "the Jew" in such Israelis, and may assume that they are "less Jewish." The lack of specificity, however, does not necessarily mean that Jewishness has a less important role in the life of Israelis.

Despite the demarcation between activities of a general American character and those which are specifically Jewish, the American and Jewish subidentities of the American Jew cannot be completely disentangled as if they were separate entities operating on different planes. The American Jew is socialized simultaneously in the overall American culture and in the subculture of his minority group. These two strands in his ethnic identity interlock and interact; he is both American *and* Jewish, his Americanism being influenced by his Jewishness and his Jewishness by his Americanism. One of the students saw it as follows: "In America I'm caught between the two currents—one of Americanism and the other of Judaism. Though they never seem to be at extremes, one must adapt to the other for a secure and compatible life." His Americanism and his Jewishness may, however, be competitively interdependent; at certain points greater adherence to the norms of the American culture may mean less adherence to the specific Jewish norms, and vice versa.[3]

By limiting the scope of his Jewishness and developing a compartmentalization between general and specifically Jewish activities, the American Jew has reduced the more obvious occasions of conflict between the two. The reduction in the scope of the Jewishness of the American Jew means in effect that the pervasive majority culture has intruded into an increasing number of areas from which the influence of the minority subculture has been ousted.[4]

Unlike Jews in the United States who live in a non-Jewish majority culture, Israelis are socialized in a culture developed by a Jewish majority. Although either the Jewish or the Israeli subidentity may be dominant, they coexist in many regions and may reinforce one another. For the Israeli Jew, "seeing himself as Israeli" does not preclude "seeing himself as Jewish." On the contrary, for many Israelis the one identity implies the other. The responses to questions put to young Israelis on the subject indicate that not only do the majority see a connection between feeling Jewish and feeling Israeli but that very few (only 4 per cent) see "feeling more Israeli" as meaning "feeling less Jewish" [5] (Tables 3 and 4).

The relationship between Israeliness and Jewishness is likely to be a source of considerable confusion to the visiting students. On the one hand, they may sense a special relationship between Israel and Jewishness, but on the other hand they may tend to view the link between the Israeli and Jewish subidentities in the terms in which they are accustomed to think of their Americanism and their Jewishness—as distinct and separate. They will find it difficult to grasp that the Israeli Jew may represent an emerging integration of Israeliness and Jewishness, with each component reinforcing the other.[6]

The Basis of Alignment

An ethnic identity aligns and marks off, and both facets need to be considered in the comparison between the Jewishness of the students and their hosts.

The "marking off" group in the American environment —the non-Jewish majority—is omnipresent. Thus in America the students are constantly reminded of their Jewishness; the juxtaposition of Jew and non-Jew heightens the awareness of their Jewishness, i.e., increases the salience of the Jewish factor.

When Israeli students are presented with the sentence

"We are Jews and they are——," the missing word they supply is generally the Hebrew equivalent of "Gentiles." [7] The Jewish majority in Israel do not see themselves as marked off by the Arab and other minorities in the country. When they do think of themselves as marked off as Jews, they perceive themselves in a world-wide context in which the marking-off group is the general category of non-Jews, non-Jews of history, at times non-Jews in a country persecuting its Jews, generally non-Jews at a distance about whose existence they can forget for periods of time. The Gentiles of that world are not immediately present as are the non-Jews whom the Jew in America encounters at every turn, and accordingly in the everyday living of the Israelis the fact of their being Jewish is thrust into the forefront of their consciousness less often than it is for members of a Jewish minority. The visiting American students may assume that the Israelis lack interest in their Jewishness. The lower awareness, or salience, does not, however, signify that their Jewishness is unattractive, i.e., lacks positive valence, for the Israelis.

We turn now to the other facet of an ethnic identity—it aligns an individual with certain others. The students will discover striking dissimilarities between themselves and the Jews of Israel. Indeed, one of the features of contemporary Jewish life is the growing dissimilarity between the Jews of Israel and American Jewry. At one time both communities were largely composed of immigrants from Europe, but the descendants of these immigrants have been socialized in very different environments. Moreover, a sizeable proportion of Israel's Jewish population is now from Oriental countries. There are marked differences not only in appearance but also in outlook and even in forms of religious practice. Coming as they probably do with a stereotyped picture of what a Jew is, the students may be taken aback by the divergence they encounter. And the question arises, how will they define their relationship to the Israelis who are so different? To what extent and on what basis—similarity, interdependence, or both—will they perceive themselves and the Israelis as sharing a common Jewish group belongingness?

An ethnic identity implies an alignment with a group across time, with its past and future. American Jews and Israelis share a common historical experience as parts of a Jewish people, and some, at least, of the members of the two communities also have a sense of common destiny. It is from this historical past that the peculiar involvement of the students in Israel stems. We may anticipate that the students will feel closest to Israelis when events from the common past are commemorated—at the time of the Festivals and on occasions such as Remembrance Day (for the martyred Jews of Europe).

Each community will, however, have a selective approach to that past. The Israelis naturally emphasize aspects of the past which fit the temper of the present—the mood of an independent people taking its destiny into its own hands. They frequently deprecate what they regard as the "passivity" of Jewish life through the centuries and the dependence of Jewish communities on the majorities among whom they dwell.

The yardstick that the Ashkenazic (European) communities in Israel use to measure Jewish activity in the Diaspora is largely based on the European experience of the Jewish people. Such Jewish life as is still maintained there is seen as having a precarious existence. The criteria employed by Israelis of the Oriental communities are based on their knowledge of countries which they had to evacuate. The views of Israelis about the future of the Diaspora are accordingly pessimistic.[8]

The views of the American students about the future are likely to diverge at some points from those of the Israelis. They will have a more optimistic outlook about the prospects of American Jewry. As proof of their potential cultural productivity, American Jews often point to the existence in the past of flourishing centers of Jewish culture —in Babylonia, in Spain, and in Eastern Europe—outside of the Land of Israel. Refusing to allow the tragic fate of so many Diaspora communities to contradict their hopes for a bright Jewish future in the United States, they are likely to indicate that "America is different."

Forms of Identification

The forms of identification in American Jewry cover a wide range—from strict religious observance to the minimal identification expressed by attendance at a religious service once a year, by a donation to a Jewish charity, or by nominal membership in a Jewish organization. In what areas of his life a Jew can be unabashedly Jewish is determined to a large extent by the prevailing culture. In the United States religious affiliation provides the most acceptable distinction between groups; the affiliation with a religious congregation is frequently an act of identification rather than an expression of religiosity.

Since the Israeli lives in a "Jewish" environment, he does not need to demonstrate his Jewish identification in the way the American Jew feels impelled to do. The American Jew expresses his Jewishness through forms of behavior which make him different from the majority around him; the Jew in Israel can be such by simply being like others in the majority.

American Jewish students visiting Israel will find themselves in a setting in which religious observance has less of an ethnic identificational function and in which Jewishness expresses itself in ways that are not always identical with those in the American environment. They may find it necessary to redefine what "being Jewish" is.

Relative Strength of Subidentities

In any given sector of American Jewry a certain balance or equilibrium exists between the forces making for conformity to the norms of the minority culture and those making for conformity to the norms of the general culture. This equilibrium differs for the various sectors, and there are, of course, individual variations within each sector. The reactions of the American Jewish students visiting Israel can be properly assessed only in the light of the balance existing at a particular time between the two constituent elements of their ethnic identity.

There has been no investigation of a representative sample of American Jewish youth with whom the students in our study could be compared, but the degree of Jewish identification which they showed was undoubtedly in excess of what may be expected from a large section of American Jewish youth.[9] The very fact of their coming to Israel indicates, as we have pointed out, a predilection in a Jewish direction.

Their responses to questions presented on board ship en route for Israel indicated that the attractiveness of their Jewishness was high. Asked whether, if they were to be born all over again, they would wish to be born Jews and also whether they would wish to be born in the United States, the response in both cases was positive, but the desire to be born Jews was more emphatic (Tables 5 and 6).

When confronted with a choice on a Jewish-American continuum, 48 per cent of the students indicated that their Jewishness had the higher potency; 17 per cent gave greater weight to their Americanism and 35 per cent placed themselves midway between the two (Table 7).

The students may tend to compare the Jewishness of the Israelis with their own. We have already indicated likely sources of confusion and misunderstanding about the Jewish identity of the Israeli. It is necessary to add that the accuracy of their assessment will also depend on whether the students take into account adequately the wide variations in Jewishness within the Israeli community or generalize on the basis of their knowledge of one particular sector.

They will find a greater measure of Jewishness among members of the older generation of Israelis as compared with the younger, and among religious youth as compared with secular youth. The religious young Israelis not only feel themselves more "Jewish" than do the nonreligious, but also their attitude to Jews everywhere is more strongly positive—although a serious concern for the fate of Jews in other countries is present in nonreligious youth as well.[10] Israeli educators have expressed anxiety about the weakening of "Jewish consciousness" among secular youth, and the American Jewish students may experience a sense of disappointment when meeting them.

CHAPTER 5

In the New Situation:
The Unfamiliar Homeland

"We will arrive in Israel in about an hour. Plan to kiss the ground. The first few moments will be strange," wrote a student in his diary. And another student reported: "I was crying. Everybody was very touched."

For some the elation of arrival in Israel was marred by Customs and other formalities:

There was so much confusion getting through Customs. You don't realize you are in Israel.

I was certain that the moment I set foot on Israeli soil I would be overwhelmed by a sense of holiness and an awareness which would never leave me that at last I was in the land of our forefathers. With all this behind me and within me I stepped onto the plane at Kennedy airport. While waiting for customs fifteen hours later at Lod I suddenly realized that the only sensations I'd been experiencing since debarkation were those of bewilderment and fatigue.

Even they, however, were caught up like the others in the intense excitement as the bus ascends the Judaean hills on the way to Jerusalem. Some of the students felt that the country to which they had come was indeed the "Promised Land."

I found the ascent to Jerusalem more beautiful than anything I had seen before. Literally I wanted to run and kiss the earth.

When I arrived I was overwhelmed, excited. The country is very beautiful. Everything is cultivated.

Their joy had an emotional intensity which far transcended the excitement of tourists or students arriving in a foreign land. As he watched them a non-Jewish student traveling with the group reflected on his comparative calm:

The main thing that I remember is that I wondered at my reaction to coming to Israel for the first time. I wondered why I did not share the enthusiasm and excitement felt by many of the other students in the group. It seemed almost routine that I should be here. Why did it not mean more to me? Moreover, I seemed to be looking through a glass that allowed me to see perfectly but separated me from any involvement in or with all that I was seeing.

As the students moved into the day-to-day life of the country, shadows crept in. Thus, one of them who spoke enthusiastically about the "tremendous experience of seeing something built from scratch," added reflectively: "But now I am coming to see more of the everyday problems rather than just the glory." The delight of being in Israel was, however, aroused afresh from time to time and, for most of them, persisted throughout the sojourn. There were frequent events, such as the festivals, which rekindled their enthusiasm. "Wonderful thing to see children and adults working together to build their 'succoth' (booths) for the coming 'chag' (festival—of Tabernacles). You see 'succoth' everywhere."

During the initial period of the sojourn the students were inclined to make facile, broad generalizations about Israel and Israelis, even though they often added, "I don't want to generalize." The discourtesy experienced at the hands of a particular cab-driver in Jerusalem could variously lead to the attribution of the quality of discourtesy to "cab-drivers" in general, or to "Jerusalemites," or to "Israelis." An incident at the Customs Office or in a theatre could trigger an exasperated comment about Israelis.

I went to pick up my package and became involved in a mess that took 2½ hours. First I was sent back to the Customs Office, on to Room 2 for cross-examination . . . and back to the parcel room which tried to send me back to No. 2. Oh, the Israelis!

Our group underwent another new experience, not with the stage but with the audience; we received our first lesson on Israeli public manners. These Israelis stole our seats, refused to give them up, then were kind enough to point out other possible locations. Such a people!

Gradually a process of differentiation set in. Instead of making the comprehensive characterizations of the first weeks, they increasingly separated out single experiences, whether good or bad, and viewed them as instances which were not necessarily typical. When the students in the panel group were reinterviewed at the end of four months in Israel and were asked about Israelis, they referred specifically to the individuals they had met, or—to the extent that they did generalize—to differentiated categories such as the *sabras* (native-born Israelis), the urban dwellers of Jerusalem, Haifa, or Tel Aviv, the members of *kibbutzim* (collective settlements) or *moshavim* (smallholders' settlements), the veteran settlers, the new immigrants, and the Oriental communities.

The reintegration or organization of the differentiated percepts was a complex matter. Early in the sojourn the students were overwhelmed by the multitude of new experiences. In the interviews they would often mention that new impressions kept "pouring in," that they could not "sort them out" properly, and that they needed an opportunity to "sit back" and "think it all through." In the later stages integration was easier, but at this point students tended to postpone attempts at organization. They were aware that more "raw data" were still coming in every day and preferred to wait for the perspective which the return home was expected to provide. This attitude was reflected in a number of the remarks that the students made in interviews conducted shortly before their departure from Israel. Thus, a student observed at the end of the interview:

Well, if you had interviewed me last week you would have gotten an entirely different impression. I've been trying to make some sense out of this year and every week it comes out differently. You ought to come and interview me after I've been home for a while.

Feelings of "At Homeness" and Strangeness

While still in the States they had often traversed Israel in their mind's eye, and the names on its map evoked many associations; yet on arrival they found themselves in an environment in which much was new and unfamiliar even to the best-informed among them. In the interviews during this period they reported feelings of both "at homeness" and strangeness. The fact that they were among Jews gave them a sense of being "at home." "I feel good all the time to think that all the people I see are Jews."

At the same time these Jews were different from the Jews they knew in the United States, and—what was least expected—their Jewishness took different forms. "I had not fully realized what I would find in Israel and all the new

47

things I encounter make me feel like a stranger among Jews. I don't seem to fit into the strange society of Israel."

They might ordinarily have found themselves closest to the sabras of their own age whose exploits they often admired. They discovered, however, that the sabras had limited understanding of the problems of the Jewish life the students had known—and apparently little curiosity about these problems. This does not mean that the sabras had no concern for the fate of Jews wherever they dwell; their concern may in fact have been no less than that possessed by the students. What dismayed the students was the failure of the sabras, who had grown up as members of a majority, to comprehend the complexities of a Diaspora minority existence. There was a consequent lack of rapport on what was for the students a matter of crucial concern.

I am disappointed with the (Israeli) students—they have no empathy with the Galuth-Jew [the Jew in the Exile] and the new immigrant.

It's hard to feel close to them. It's difficult for them to understand people from "chutz la'aretz" [outside of Israel].

Tonight I attempted to explain to Leah and Yehuda the difference between Orthodox and Conservative Judaism. Leah, being a sabra, couldn't understand the position of Jews in "chutz la'aretz." It's unfortunate that such a situation exists but how can someone understand that which is entirely beyond the realm of his experience.

Since the older settlers, mainly from Eastern Europe, had this understanding, and possibly because they reminded many of their own parents or grandparents, the students felt closer to them than to the sabras. In relation to them, however, there were age and other differences.

The students found most familiar, and felt closest to, settlers with backgrounds like their own—those from the
United States and other English-speaking countries (Table
8). "If somewhere in the vicinity I hear somebody speak
with an English accent, I'm drawn to him. I feel I can ask
an Anglo-Saxon about my problems because he's more like
me."

The students sympathized with the plight of the new immigrants, many of whom had arrived destitute. In spite of
their compassion, they found it difficult to develop a sense
of closeness to the immigrants, whether from the European
or Oriental countries (Table 8). There was always a conscious effort on their part not to discriminate between these
two groups, and they were indignant about any sign of
prejudice against the Oriental sector. In the interviews,
however, some students indicated how taken aback they
were to see how sharply the immigrants from the Orient
differed from the picture the word "Jew" had hitherto conjured up for them. Their explanations were given somewhat guiltily:

I regard about all Jews as my kith and kin regardless of where
they live but I cannot truthfully regard many of the Eastern
people as my brethren.

I had greater rapport with people from the West. In my contact with the Eastern Jews I always felt I can help them, and
can't get anything from them.

The more religiously inclined had hoped to find a common bond with Israelis in religious observance. The
Orthodox students, and also some of the Conservatives, did
succeed in establishing the desired link with the religious
circles with whom they came into contact. But the Reform

students and a number of the Conservatives found themselves out of accord with forms of religious practice and with a religious outlook which differed from what they had been accustomed to in the United States. They could locate, when they so wished, a Conservative or Reform Congregation, but there they could discover few native Israeli youth. (The great majority of religious Israeli students attend Orthodox services.) Many of the Americans, Orthodox and others, were drawn to the services conducted by the Israeli students at the Hillel House and the participation in these services with Israelis did indeed emphasize their common Jewishness. But the non-Orthodox among them remained aware of an element of strangeness, commenting in particular on the *mechitza* (the seating apart of male and female).

The students were moreover taken aback by the intensity of the friction generated by religious issues in the country and by the absence of what they termed a middle ground. "Here you are either religious or nothing" was a remark frequently heard.

Although the particular variations in religious practice with which they were familiar in their American environment are obviously absent in Israel, many of the students failed to observe such diversity as does exist among Israeli religious groups. Only a few spent any appreciable time at a religious kibbutz. They also tended to underestimate the extent of religious observance in Israel. In the interviews they were asked to estimate the percentage of observant Jews in Israel's population; the median estimate was 10 per cent, whereas in fact the percentage is at least three times that figure.[1]

Accustomed as they were to religious expressions of Jewish identification in the United States, the students found difficulty at the outset of their visit in categorizing nonreligious Israelis. The nonreligious students among the Americans welcomed the possibility of a Jewish identification without religious commitment, but even they somehow felt that Israelis should be "more Jewish." Those students who thought of their own Jewishness in exclusively religious terms were the most disconcerted and began to find it necessary to reorganize their conception of what "being Jewish" could mean. "I am constantly struck by my new realization of my own Jewishness as being largely cultural (like feeling a need to identify Jewishly when in the U.S.) whereas I once mistook this attitude for a really religious approach."

Although some of the students on arrival in Israel could converse in Hebrew, others had the merest smattering of a knowledge. One of the situations in which these students felt themselves strangers was when they were in the company of Israelis and found themselves unable to understand the Hebrew.[2] "When I am with a group of Israelis who are speaking Hebrew rapidly I feel like I don't belong because there is a lack of communication."

Their attitude toward Hebrew paralleled their feelings about Israel. It was the language of their people and not a foreign tongue, but at the same time a language with which they were only vaguely familiar. On the ship they expressed highly positive feelings about Hebrew. After the months of struggle in Israel with the complexities of the language, some of them were less enthusiastic, but the attitude of the group as a whole was still positive (Table 9).[3]

The Stranger Group

Already on board ship en route to Israel the students rapidly "became a group," as they phrased it, even though most of them had no previous acquaintance with one another. Away from their accustomed surroundings they experienced the need for peer-group contact more strongly than ever and as participants in the same program they naturally drew together.

The mutual attraction was strengthened in Jerusalem. Whereas Israelis were part of the unfamiliar new situation, the Americans represented the familiar. They had the same background and were passing through the same experiences. They were all in the position of being in Israel for a year of study and so had a similar frame of reference for their experiences, a similar need to come to a temporary *modus vivendi* with the Israeli host society. On a number of issues the credibility of Israeli sources of information was suspect. Some students predicted on arrival that there would be attempts by the Israelis to "convert" or "propagandize" them, but they harbored no such suspicions about their countrymen.

The American student group became a clearinghouse for experiences and impressions, supplying its members with needed information and the verification of information received from other sources. Our observers found it revealing to watch the students returning from their first weekend vacation. Each student delivered a detailed report of his experiences, and his friends did not confine themselves to passive listening. In these "bull-sessions" the events were analyzed: "O.K. . . . but that's not typical" or "well that's because . . ." were frequent remarks during these exchanges. A report was only the beginning of a conversation; almost invariably a discussion followed in which experiences were compared and evaluated. As a student wrote in his diary: "The greatest thing in returning from *chofesh* [vacation] is seeing the excitement of the kids and hearing their experiences." A significant feature of these excursions was thus the subsequent setting-into-context provided by the discussions in the stranger group. Speaking of what the group meant to him, a student remarked: "It helped to temper first impressions, it provided a sounding board for thoughts on Israel."

During the months that they attended the ulpan (before the commencement of the university academic year) they were housed in the same dormitories, took meals together, and at times went on joint excursions into the country. Later when university studies began and they shared rooms with Israeli students they were not in such constant physical proximity. The initial high frequency of reference to the group persisted, however, in a number of forms throughout the year. Almost all the students reported that their closest friendships remained with their fellow-Americans (Table 8). On the campus it was noticeable that the American students were always to be seen in each other's company; the stranger group had something of the quality of a family relationship.

When they were asked the advantages of coming to Israel as a member of an organized group, most students indicated the sense of security given them by the group in the new environment. "It enabled me to form friendships— gave me some security—when I most felt alone and a stranger." And again, "It has given me a feeling of security at a time when I absolutely needed it."

The close contact with their own countrymen, who represented a wide variety of religious and nonreligious viewpoints, incidentally had another outcome which the students amusedly recognized—it enabled them to learn much about American Jews. "It was a unique chance to live close to and learn about a select and specific group of American Jews." "I have had that many more opportunities to observe Americans not in America and that many more opportunities to discuss views."

CHAPTER 6

Strangers among Kinsfolk: The Problem of Social Contact

The American Jewish students who came to Israel looked upon themselves as different from the general mass of strangers sojourning among foreign hosts. They saw their hosts as kinsfolk; [1] the great majority (83 per cent) regarded Jews of all countries as "kith and kin" (Table 34). Although their position remained essentially that of strangers, this kinship did arouse special expectations on both sides. Observing their peculiar involvement in Israel, one of the non-Jewish students living with the group in the dormitory observed:

I do not feel the ties and the kinship with Israel that so many of the Jewish students feel. I regard Israel as a fascinating place to study, learn and experience things that cannot be experienced in most places in the world. But I, of course, do not regard Israel as home or even as a primary focal point in my religious experience. As a result, I do not feel many of the same pressures felt by my fellow-students.

The students did not anticipate any insurmountable difficulty in getting to know their Israeli hosts. Their expectation was that as Jews meeting fellow-Jews they would enjoy a more privileged position than mere strangers in a foreign country. The area of social contact, however, proved to be beset—for them—with unforeseen complications.

What did the students have in mind when they spoke of contact with Israelis? The term "contact" holds many meanings. A casual exchange of greetings in the bus or the grocery shop, discussion of the future of American Jewry, a social gathering—all of these can be termed "contacts" but would be expected to have quite different effects in terms of the involvement of the parties in the contact and the tension or satisfaction created. Cook and Selltiz have distinguished between two dimensions of the contact situation, namely its "acquaintance potential," i.e., the opportunity it provides for the participants to "get to know" one another, and its "social acceptance implication," i.e., the extent to which the contact implies that the one participant is willing to accept the other as a social equal and at least potentially as a friend.[2] When the students spoke of "contact with Israelis," they meant contact with a high acquaintance potential and preferably also with an implication of social acceptance.

The students began their stay in Israel in relative isolation, living and studying with fellow-strangers before the start of the university academic year. In this period, contact of any depth was rarely established between the students and Israelis. Casual contacts did take place with Israelis in shops, buses, and offices, and when the students were traveling outside of Jerusalem during weekends they met a variety of people. Although most of these contacts were of a fleeting, superficial kind, they sufficed to give the students the feeling that they were being introduced into the life of the country and its people. They were, moreover, grateful for such hospitality as was extended them. The closer contacts were usually established with relatives and with American settlers.

The superficiality of the contacts did not disturb the visitors during the first two months when they were fully occupied absorbing new impressions. But it became clear that they would not rest content with this; what they wanted was a deeper acquaintanceship, preferably friendship, permitting them to get closer to Israelis and to learn to understand them and their way of life. They were interested in meeting, in particular, Israelis of their own age, and so they began speaking with eager anticipation of the time when they would share a room with an Israeli student and would meet students on the campus.

With the opening of the university year the students entered a situation with higher acquaintance potential. They were now sharing rooms with Israeli students, and could meet Israeli students in the dormitories and classrooms. Relations with the Israeli roommates were generally good and through them they often met other Israelis.

Despite this change, a sense of disappointment increasingly crept into their reports about the nature of the social contact with the Israeli students. They found to their dismay that they were not succeeding in establishing close relationships with young Israelis. Their disappointment was all the keener because of their expectation that the common Jewishness would serve as a basis for more intimate friendship with their hosts. Some students reacted with sorrow, others, with indignation.

If you passed them on the campus during the week they usually would not answer your timid little smile of recognition. At a cafeteria table Israelis had the art of never making eye contact with their fellow eater-across-the-table to whom they'd never-been-introduced down to perfection.

My contact with Israelis was almost non-existent for a good while even after I had sufficient time to get to know them. I will state bluntly that this is because they do not comprise the easiest society to become a member of or know intimately, are clannish and keep to themselves; facts to which any foreigner who has tried to make contact with them will testify.

What were the barriers to social contact of the kind desired by the students?

In the first place, cultural differences bedeviled relations. The students expected that acquaintanceship would be established in the way to which they were accustomed in the United States. Israelis, however, do not initiate contact with strangers with the relative ease with which Americans do. Although on the whole they were friendly, they usually did not go out of their way to initiate contact. On the other hand, the students who saw themselves as the guests and the Israelis as the hosts waited for the Israelis to take the initiative. Their expectations were not met. The students had some awareness that many Israeli cultural patterns differ from the American. What they did not adequately grasp, however, was that the very process of getting acquainted with this people differs from that to which they were accustomed in the United States.[3]

Israelis, moreover, are less expansive and effusive in extending greetings and invitations. Thus the students were on occasion at a loss to interpret social cues in their new environment. Observers watching the social contacts between students and members of a kibbutz at which they were staying commented on the difficulties the students experienced in interpreting the behavior of their hosts. A member of the kibbutz who had been working with a student would propose, in a manner which seemed off-hand or casual to the student, that the latter "drop into my room sometimes for tea." The student would thank him but would not go—not because he did not want to, but because "I really don't know whether he wanted me to come. He just said it as if it was something to be said." In other words, since the invitation lacked the customary American expansive courtesy, the student did not know how to interpret it. On the other hand, the members of the kibbutz too suffered from this cultural misunderstanding. A member in charge of arrangements for the students commented to an observer: "They just keep to themselves. . . . Quite a lot of us have invited them for tea—but they don't come."

Even when acquaintanceship was established, social acceptance into student circles did not readily follow, in part because of the nature of the circles on the university campus in Israel. The student in a small country such as Israel finds on the campus old acquaintances from his days at High School or in the Army. The circles formed on the basis of these associations and the common experiences and memories that go with them are not easily penetrable by the stranger; even if he is allowed inside, he feels out of place. Indeed, it was easier for an American student to meet Israeli students singly than within one of these circles. In interviews, some of the students who had Israeli roommates indicated that they felt themselves outsiders when the Israeli roommate's friends happened to assemble in the room. "My roommate had all her friends from Rehovot. They had been to school together. I felt as if I didn't belong in my own room."

There is also less of a leisurely campus life at the Hebrew University than at the universities from which the American students come. The Israeli students commence their university studies after the maturing experience of two and a half (now, three) years in the Army, which they enter on matriculation (even the girls render two years' service); many of them work to earn a living while pursuing their studies, and they accordingly have less time for extra-curricular activities.

Some of the students clung to the illusion that the barrier to the desired social contact was their ignorance of Hebrew. With time the increased command of Hebrew did extend the range of communication possibilities and made acquaintanceship easier, but it did not necessarily bring social acceptance in its wake.

The kind of deep and enduring contact for which the students were eager is generally built around mutual interests. The common Jewishness of the American and Israeli students might have been supposed to serve not only as a bond but as the basis for a continuing dialogue. Although one reason the visiting American students were interested in establishing contact with their hosts was precisely to learn all they could about the life of the country and its people, the Israeli students did not have a similar curiosity about the American Jewish community. A visiting stranger anywhere is likely to be more interested in his hosts and their form of life than they are in him and in his background. The Israeli students were not uninterested, but in the daily round of their lives they did not care to give much thought to the subject of American Jewry.

The religious Israeli students, who stood out as a cohesive observant minority, welcomed the Orthodox American students who joined them at the synagogue and in a variety of celebrations; the joint religious observances constituted a bond transcending the American-Israeli difference. The custom of inviting guests for one of the Sabbath meals is widely observed, and here Israeli families took the initiative. The Orthodox students were the most frequent beneficiaries of such hospitality. The contact on the Sabbath when everyone concerned had leisure sometimes developed into friendship.

The Ambivalence of the Israeli Hosts

How did the Israeli hosts regard their student guests?

In at least one important aspect the Israelis viewed the students in a way hosts in other countries do not think of the foreign students in their midst. Israeli society is comparable to an open and incomplete group.[4] Jews in other parts of the world are considered potential members and by a special statute, "The Law of the Return," they are admitted to Israel as by right and are immediately accorded citizenship. There is much concern that only a relatively small proportion have come to settle from lands in which Jews live in freedom. In the view of Israelis many more American Jews should have chosen to come. When they meet American Jewish students they look at them hopefully as desirable members for the group, but at the same time they are aware that the chances of their returning eventually as settlers are slim, whatever their protestations may be. Traces of ambivalence accordingly appear in the attitude of the hosts.

This ambivalence may be said to characterize Israeli society as a whole and exists as a background setting overlapping the specific contact situations. At the same time some sections of this society are more ready than others for day-to-day social contact with strangers. The students at the Institute at one stage of their sojourn went to work in kibbutzim and were dispersed among nine such settlements. The settlements were classified as "open," "indifferent," and "closed" according to the replies of the students to the following question: Which of the following statements best characterizes the attitude of the kibbutz members toward your group? Open: (1) they went out of their way to make us feel at home; (2) they helped in creating contact. Indifferent: (3) they didn't do much in particular to establish contact, but were willing, if we took the initiative; (4) they were somewhat reticent, but if we really tried, we succeeded in establishing contact. Closed: (5) they didn't care much for having contact with us beyond what was necessary during work; (6) they didn't care at all for having contact with us.

This classification was validated by comments of the students in interviews and in their diaries. Thus, a student at a closed kibbutz reported: "The kibbutz didn't accept us. In the dining-hall all of us [students] sat together. In the evenings we didn't dare to go and visit the [kibbutz] members." And, "The attitude of the kibbutz to us was cool." The students at the open kibbutzim spoke enthusiastically: "The members received us with open arms. In all the houses they received us. They linked us to them quite informally." And, "The relations [with kibbutz members] were close— they want young people."

A student who stayed at an indifferent kibbutz and had occasion to visit an open one remarked: "I can't seem to grasp the idea that so many people go out of their way to talk to you here." The initial situation at the indifferent kibbutzim is rather clearly stated by the student who reports: "The members expect us to just walk into their houses and visit them and so they wait for us to make the first move. But we feel odd just barging in." A few weeks later, however, after this student had reached the conclusion that "the time has come to try to get to know more [kibbutz members]," she can state, "I have gotten to know practically everyone," and still later she comments, "All of a sudden many people have done about faces (including the woman who never smiles)."

The satisfaction or dissatisfaction subsequently expressed with the stay at the settlement correlated with its openness or closedness. The students in the open settlements were the most positive in their attitudes to the settlement and its members.

The students were provided with the greatest amount of explicit information in the open settlements; in the others they had to rely more on their own observation. Although they participated in the work situation in all the settlements, their opportunities for participation outside of work existed mainly in the open settlements. Thus, in one of these settlements a plan was implemented whereby a number of families each "adopted" a student for the duration of his stay, inviting him frequently for visits and treating him as a member of the family. The students in the interviews frequently referred with enthusiasm to what they had learned from their participant roles in the family. In these instances the Israeli family has ceased to be for them an exhibit viewed from the outside.

As for the American students at the Hebrew University, the Israelis they met on the campus belonged mainly to the indifferent category, and little progress was made during the year in establishing social contact with them. Occasionally a student would encounter off campus—on a visit to a kibbutz or to an Israeli family for a Sabbath meal—a group which was open and he would record his delight at the warmth of the reception he was accorded.

The Failure to be Accepted

There were, of course, individual differences in the degree of success achieved in social relations. A number of the girls were dated by Israeli boys. But the majority of students did not succeed in establishing anything beyond superficial acquaintanceship with their Israeli peers and they were bitterly disappointed at their failure to be accepted into Israeli social circles.

In the United States they had known that not all social groups were open to them. But to the extent that these barriers resulted from their ethnic identity, they arose from their being Jewish. Their American subidentity obviously did not bar them from acceptance in American groups. The students had therefore developed a "perceptual readiness" to view their Jewishness as a barrier but had not thought of their Americanism in that light. When they came to Israel they felt that this was the society in which their Jewishness no longer would be a handicap and indeed would be the key to their acceptance. While they met with no discrimination, the social encounter with Israelis was complicated by an unexpected factor. They were not just Jews meeting other Jews, but American strangers confronting their Israeli hosts. For their Americanism to constitute a barrier was for them a novel experience. "Ironically, while at home I always felt myself slightly different from 'Americans,' here my 'Americanism' makes me different in a similar way from 'Israelis.' "

The reactions of the students to nonacceptance in Israeli circles differed. In a number of cases it resulted in withdrawal—a falling-back upon the stranger-group for their social contacts and reassurance. These students identified even more strongly with the other Americans and reconciled themselves to the role of stranger in the host society. The following statement by one such student echoes the reactions of many others: "At the beginning I thought it would require no particular effort to make friends, but when I saw the Israelis weren't interested I began to stick with the Americans. Most of them had decided the same, so we all stayed together."

This was indeed a course of least resistance often followed. A number of the students confessed that the shelter and companionship so readily available in the American student group made them less persistent in the search for Israeli friends. "The closeness developed among the group in the summer keeps many of us from going outside to meet Israelis and develop close relationships with Israelis."

Another type of response occurred among a few of the students. Their Americanism, perceived as a barrier to acceptance, acquired a negative valence and they rejected not the Israelis but their fellow-Americans. They attempted to disassociate themselves from the other strangers in order to be seen by the Israelis as different from these others.

As a big group of Americans I think we are regarded by Israelis more negatively than if we came as individual students.

I don't like being labeled as a member of an "American" group. . . . The character of American youth in general doesn't appeal to me.

A further example of this type of response occurred in a kibbutz where students from the Institute on arrival found another group of young Americans already installed. When the new arrivals discovered the difficulties in getting close to the members of the kibbutz they decided the reason was the "distorted picture of Americans" created by the previous group. The diaries and interviews with the students contained numerous complaints that the members of the kibbutz "don't differentiate between them (the first group) and us." They insisted on being separated from the others.

Subsequently friction arose within the group of students because the members of the kibbutz "judged all of us as one." The stranger group began to lose cohesiveness, each stranger rejecting others in the effort to be accepted by the hosts.

The difficulties in social contact left the students with an unfavorable view of the social graces of Israelis. They appreciated the hospitality accorded in some kibbutzim and homes; on the Semantic Differential Israelis were rated higher on this trait toward the end of the sojourn than they were while the students were en route to Israel. But on the other social contact variables the students rated Israelis less favorably than at the outset. Israelis were seen as less "courteous," less "warm," less "sociable" (Table 52).

Despite these disappointments, the students still left with a favorable impression of Israel and with a feeling of satisfaction about the sojourn. This was due in part to the distinction they drew between Israel and Israelis, but would also indicate that there may be factors other than social contact which shape the impression of the sojourn.

When satisfying social contact can be achieved, however, it seems to produce more favorable attitudes to the host country. Using some of the questionnaire items developed in our study, Hofman and Zak compared the reactions of visiting American students who established varying degrees of social contact with Israeli students at Kfar Hayarok, a rural school complete with its own small campus. They found that high contact was associated with favorable attitude change.[5]

Learning from the Hosts

Under what circumstances, in their contact with Israeli hosts, were the students influenced by what they heard from them?

On matters relating to Israel, they recognized that the superior knowledge of their hosts qualified them to be authoritative informants. But as strangers located on the periphery of Israeli society without access to the center, they were wary of accepting the opinions of their hosts without question. The views of the hosts were often reexamined within the stranger group.

On problems of general interest affecting the Jewish people as a whole, the students were more ready to accept the views of Israelis; in such cases the students felt a sense of "we-ness" or common group belongingness with the hosts.[6] Indeed to the extent that the host was perceived as "one of us," he was more likely to succeed as an agent of change. The boundaries of the in-group were redrawn each time in accordance with the particular situation. In regard to some issues the Israeli hosts were seen primarily in terms of their Jewish role as "insiders"; in relation to other issues they remained just Israelis and "outsiders."

When Israelis criticized American life and character, the students immediately rose to the defense and disdainfully rejected the views of "outsiders." To criticisms of American foreign policy they did not object. They often subscribed to these criticisms, and even when they did not, they recognized the legitimacy of criticism of a policy which affected the outside world. But attacks on the American way of life aroused strong emotions. "They just don't know what they are talking about," "I can't stand them lecturing to me" were frequent comments. No less emphatic was the rejection of the prophecies expressed by some Israelis about a tide of antisemitism likely to engulf American Jewry at some time in the future. The students were prepared to have another American raise the problem, but when an Israeli did so the response was uniformly negative. They were apparently ready to enquire into the validity of this prediction with persons sharing the same American-Jewish identity and the same value-system, but when it was propounded by "outsiders" the reaction was one of indignant dissent. When Israelis linked this warning about the future to the question "Why don't you immigrate to Israel?" the students reacted with a defense of their position rather than with a readiness to examine the validity of the challenge. Indeed, their hosts' attempts to influence them failed when the students felt they were being subjected to pressure.

The students seemed more open to influence by what they saw of their hosts in action than by what the hosts told them. Thus, a counselor's ready response to the call for military service in a crisis made a deeper impression as an exemplification of the spirit of the people than his numerous discussions with them.

CHAPTER 7

In Overlapping Situations:
The Changing Salience of an Ethnic Role

The students were Americans, they were Jews, and they were temporarily—and some of them planned to be permanently—members of the Israeli community. During the year they found themselves frequently changing from one role to the other. In the new environment there were often no easily recognizable clues to the appropriateness of a particular role.

One of the students, describing in her diary her meeting with four American Gentile students, members of the 4-H Club, reflected the shift from role to role in overlapping situations:

I arrived at X [the cooperative settlement] and found a special treat: four American youth exchange students! Oh, were they Gentiles! So American looking, equipped with Southern drawls and farm hospitality spirit. Really, they were such wonderful kids and such tremendous representatives of American youth, such terrific Gentiles to enter a Jewish country. And it is good to see Gentiles occasionally, for *we* sometimes forget *they* exist and our world becomes confused and even foggy. This evening we saw each other's slides, X's and the four aitches . . . I was translating for the four aitches . . . [the following day] I spent a great deal of time talking with the four aitches and after D [a member of the settlement] showed us the place, everybody talked the subject of Israel out, from the standpoint of *American viewpoints*, then answered their questions from an *American Jew's viewpoint*, and the whole time was very valuable. This evening *all five Americans* met with the youth of X and had quite a successful evening. (Italics added.)

The initial period with its novelty of being in a Jewish country surrounded by other Jews heightened their consciousness of being Jewish. As the sojourn progressed, however, the novelty waned; no juxtaposition of Jews and non-Jews kept reminding them of their Jewishness as it had in the United States. Thirty-eight per cent reported that they had less occasion to think of themselves as Jews in Israel, although for others there were factors in a Jewish environment which continued to maintain the high salience of their Jewishness (Table 10). The following remarks reflect the differing perceptions:

In the U.S. when you are constantly in contact with Gentiles the question continually comes up. You are constantly aware of the fact that you are Jewish in the U.S. and you always wonder does the other person know, should I let on, etc. In Israel you assume most people are Jewish—so everything starts on that basis.

In the U.S. I thought of myself as a Jew, as opposed to the Gentile world. Here, on about the same occasions, I think of myself as a Jew, as part of the Jewish people.

I awaken every morning to the view of the Judaean hills and can't forget that I am in Israel—as a Jew.

While the salience of the Jewish factor receded for a number of the students, the great majority became more conscious of their Americanism. As soon as the students left

the shores of the United States and came into contact with
non-Americans they assumed the role of American representatives. They were easily identifiable and were constantly turned to as informants on American affairs. "I am
recognized as an American and treated accordingly. People
speak English to me, ask me questions about America."
Much that they had previously assumed to be universal
they now recognized to be specifically American.

Differences in standards of living, in ways of doing things and
in ways of thinking constantly confronted us. . . . We could
now see how American culture had influenced our ways of
thinking and our values and we now consciously perceived
many facets of American society that we had before taken
very much for granted.

Here my "normal American reactions" are not necessarily
normal reactions and I see more alternatives to them.

They heard frequent criticism of the United States and of
Americans, and in all such cases, if the criticism appeared in
any way unjust or unfounded, they would rise indignantly
to the defense—as Americans.

During this year I defended the U.S. more than I've done all
my life . . . against statements which were made without
knowledge or justification.

I almost never think of myself as American in America but in
Israel I often feel part of the American "we" as opposed to the
Israeli "they." Often I find I must defend America to Israelis.

How They Believe the Israelis Perceive Them

The attitude of the Israelis toward them—as the students
perceived it—heightened the salience of their Americanism.

The students had seen their Jewishness as the bond between Israelis and themselves and stressed this factor whenever they wished to be accepted into the Israeli society in which they sojourned as strangers. When asked on board the ship how they would prefer Israelis to see them—"first and foremost" as Jews or as Americans—the great majority (76 per cent) indicated that they would wish to be seen as Jews. They were accordingly disappointed to discover—this was the impression gained by 86 per cent of them—that Israelis saw them primarily as Americans (Tables 11 and 12).

Although in specific situations they were indeed seen as Americans, they may have been misperceiving the Israelis' overall view. Thus, when a psychology class at the Hebrew University were asked how they saw the American Jewish students, the majority (60 per cent) indicated that they saw them first and foremost as Jews (Table 13). In terms of what is known about impression formation [1] it was to be expected that what would be salient in the perception of Israeli students would be the quality which distinguished the visitors from others in the environment, namely their Americanism. The fact that a considerable percentage nonetheless saw them first and foremost as Jews may indicate the importance the Israelis attached to the special relationship which united them with the visitors.[2]

The impression gained by American students, however, was that they were seen first and foremost as Americans. They in turn perforce saw their hosts first and foremost as Israelis although they would have preferred to see them as Jews (Tables 14 and 15).

The students became acutely aware of the juxtaposition, new to them, of Americans and Israelis. The salience of their Americanism increased, 79 per cent declaring that they had occasion to think of themselves as Americans either "more often" or "very much more often" in Israel than in the United States (Table 16).

Changes in Valence

The valence of their Americanism, however, made no parallel increase. Some of them became more aware of desirable qualities in their American environment, but counter-influences were at play. The students found the attitude of their hosts toward America and Americans on the whole friendly but critical; the comparison with Israel at times reflected unfavorably on America—even though they often defended the country against criticism. "Being in Israel we were more able through our own comparisons with Israeli society and by taking into account the criticisms we heard from Israelis to look more critically and objectively at American life as a whole."

A different development took place in regard to their Jewishness. Although for some students its salience decreased, its valence, on the other hand, increased for most of them. The students now lived in an environment in which Jews were not in a minority and no stigma was attached to being Jewish; on the contrary, the Jewishness they shared with Israelis was seen as the passport to Israeli society. Their Jewishness thus became more attractive to them. In an interview at the conclusion of the year's sojourn (with approximately half of the student group), 61 per cent reported an increase in their sense of pride in being Jews, whereas 26 per cent indicated an increase in their pride in being Americans (Table 17).

At the end of the sojourn the students felt more strongly American than before they came, and as strongly Jewish as at the start of their sojourn. The potency of the Jewish factor, however, remained the greater (Tables 18 and 19).

73

Situational Variations

The oscillation was not just between the American and Jewish roles. Israeli society became a source of reference and the students could on occasion feel themselves approximating an Israeli role. The following question was put to find which roles were adopted in various situations.

During your stay in Israel there are situations in which you may see yourself primarily as Jewish, in some primarily as American, in some primarily as a resident of Israel. How do you think you would see yourself in the following situations; how do you think those you are in contact with see you, and how would you like them to see you?

The item "how you see yourself" was intended to establish the relative potencies of the three roles; "how you would like them to see you," the valences. The response to "how they see you" in the various situations was regarded as one of the determinants of salience. The situations included their contacts with Israeli students, American tourists, and new immigrants, and also their correspondence with non-Jews and with Jewish friends in America and with their families (Table 20).

In contact with Israeli students they would have liked to be seen as residents of Israel or as Jewish (each of these roles would have constituted a bond between them and the Israelis), least of all as Americans. They believed, however, that the Israeli students saw them primarily as Americans; thus in their contact with these students they perforce now viewed themselves as Americans.

When they encountered American tourists, the latter tended to see them as Americans, but the students disregarded this view. They were anxious to establish a distance between their role and that of the tourists; in terms of normative function the tourists served as a negative reference category. At the same time the tourists were a source of comparative reference; by contrast with the tourist paying a fleeting visit and often displaying an ignorance of conditions in Israel, they felt entitled to see themselves primarily as residents of Israel. They did not want to be mistaken for tourists.

When I meet people from abroad—Americans too—then I feel particular identification with Israel. Then I feel a part of Israel, a veteran who can give the information and help them to get oriented. Then I don't feel so much American.

At the peak of the tourist season, when Jerusalem is crowded with American visitors, I found myself speaking Hebrew with friends in public and trying not to make myself conspicuous as an American. When tourists came to the University and snapped pictures of us lounging on the grass between ulpan classes thinking we were Israeli students, we were secretly delighted and therefore did not bother to inform them of their error.

When meeting new immigrants they would have liked to reduce the distance and to have the immigrants view them in terms of the common denominator—their Jewishness. But the attention of the immigrants was riveted on what distinguishes the students from others in the environment —their Americanism. And the students divided up between those who became reconciled to seeing themselves as the immigrants see them—as Americans—and those who persisted in seeing themselves as Jews. When some of the students, however, served as teachers or youth counselors to immigrant groups they reported that they felt "really Israeli." In this situation, as in the contact with tourists, the students were able to represent Israel, in the sense that their knowledge of Israel was superior to that of the other party in the interaction.

In correspondence with non-Jews in America they re-entered the situation in which they were in juxtaposition with the marking-off group. They felt they were seen by the non-Jews primarily as Jewish (more so than by any of the other groups) and they saw themselves as such. The figures in the "Jewish" column in Table 20 (on salience, valence, and potency) are higher in the confrontation with non-Jews than in the meeting with any of the other groups.

In correspondence with family and Jewish friends the majority preferred to be seen as either Jewish or residents of Israel and saw themselves primarily as such.

Although roles shifted according to the demands of the situation, what was most "basic" to the ethnic behavior of this group of students was their Jewish identity. The students were not just Jews; they were American Jews. But it was their Jewish minority group membership which was their distinctive badge in the American environment in which they grew up. And in the development of their sense of ego-identity—which Erikson has spoken of as an integration of all identifications [3]—their relation to their minority group was the crucial constituent. As far as these students were concerned, the balance between "Jewish" and "American" on the Jewish-American scale was on the Jewish side (Table 7; cf. also Tables 5 and 6). The interviews with them showed even more clearly that the majority saw themselves as American *Jews* rather than as Jewish *Americans*. When asked in a general way about the relative strength of the two components in their ethnic identity, some students hesitated to reply because they felt they could not disentangle the elements for the purposes of this abstract comparison. (When presented with the Jewish-American scale such students tended to choose the midpoint.) Specific situations, however, would bring to the fore one facet of their identity rather than the other; in situations where both were relevant the dominance of the Jewish identity became discernible.

We suggest that in the context of our present discussion identity may be conceived of as a "latent position" which together with the situational potencies of competing roles determines behavior. In view of the primacy of the Jewish component in the identity of the students we can predict a tendency toward Jewish role-behavior in all situations of ethnic role conflict where Jewishness has any relevance.

An additional reason existed for the frequent assumption of the Jewish role by the students. Cross-pressures in some situations may render functional a "compromise role," which is legitimate in its own right and includes parts of both conflicting roles. Thus a person may "seek a compromise position by which he attempts to conform in part, though not wholly, to one or more sets of role expectations in the hope that the sanctions applied will be minimal." [4] The assumption of the Jewish role was particularly functional in the overlapping situation in which the students found themselves in Israel. To take the Israeli role would often have meant the rejection of the American one, and vice-versa. On the other hand, the Jewish role—apart from the other reasons which existed for its assumption—allowed for preserving the link to America as well as to Israel. There is minimal loss associated with taking the "compromise role." It has been shown that in cases of cross-pressure where the potencies of the American and Israeli roles approach equality, the students tend to adopt the Jewish role. [5]

CHAPTER 8

The Time Perspective
of the Sojourner

What goals did the students set for the sojourn? At what
developmental stage in their lives did they come to Israel?
What were the implications of a sojourn bounded by the
limited time span of a year? And in their appraisal of Israel
did they go beyond the particular moment in time in which
they encountered the host society and see it in a historical
perspective? The sojourn experience cannot be properly assessed without reference to these questions which relate to
the time perspective of the sojourner.

The Goals of the Sojourner

As we have already seen, most of the students had not
come to Israel primarily to study; they came to see the
country and its people. On the whole, they felt satisfaction
with their year of studies at the University, but when they
were called upon to review their impressions of the sojourn, the references were to their reactions to Israel and Israelis, to the impact of the stay on their view of themselves
and of their Jewishness, and rarely was their spontaneous
mention of their studies.

For some of the students there was the additional question of whether Israel was a country in which they could
permanently settle, and they eagerly sought out experiences

which might aid them in the making of so crucial a decision. So one such student, writing in his diary on the eve of the departure for Israel, mapped out his goal: "Must also settle for myself whether or not I want Israel. The decision must finally be made. Then with that decision made, as early as possible, to decide on what to do with my life in my decided surrounding. Decide what and where to study." And another student wrote simply: "I came to Israel to make sure whether it was the place for me."

A Period of Exploration

The students, in their late teens or their very early twenties, were in an impressionable period of their lives, exploring, testing out, easily roused to enthusiasm and equally easily disenchanted. Except for the few Rabbinical students, they had not yet decided upon professional careers and some of them sought through the experiences of their stay to clarify for themselves the direction their occupational choice should take. For almost all of them the visit was an exploration—with some more expressly articulated, with others less so—of what Israel could mean to them in their life as Jews. On the one hand, the fluidity of their plans for the future—the lack of commitment to a career or marriage—made them open to influences in their new environment, but on the other hand, the uncertainty of what was in store for them beyond their transient role as students militated against far-reaching, binding decisions.

The Limited Time-Span of the Sojourn

The foreign student is a temporary sojourner; the time for the achievement of his goals in the host society is limited and he intends to return to his home-country. In describing the time sequences of the sojourn, several of the studies in cross-cultural education have distinguished among various phases in the student's adjustment.[1]

First comes the "spectator" phase when the student, freshly arrived, is, like the tourist, an onlooker—curiously viewing and generally enjoying the novel experiences in a new environment. Even in later phases he remains at many points a spectator, continuing to view events with the detachment of an observer for whom they have only a limited relevance. The spheres in which the American Jewish students were merely spectators in Israel were fewer than is usual for students in a foreign land. Their identification as Jews with Israel precluded the dispassionate approach of the spectator. There was an indignation about things that were not in order which went beyond the irritation a visitor from the outside might experience, and at the same time an elation about praiseworthy phenomena they encountered.

Next follows what has been termed the "involvement" phase—we prefer to call it the "engagement" phase [2]—when the student can no longer remain an onlooker but must undertake his tasks within the host culture. At this time he generally encounters difficulties, and the elation of the spectator phase may be followed by a sinking of spirits. In the third, the "coming-to-terms" phase, some *modus vivendi*, or equilibrium, is established.

In the "engagement" and "coming-to-terms" phases the student continues to be influenced by the feeling that after a certain period he will disengage himself from the host culture. He is aware of the impermanence of most of the relationships he establishes in the host culture, and while he goes through the throes of adjustment he remembers that the *modus vivendi* he is called upon to establish is a temporary expedient. Thus, an experience which may be highly disconcerting to the immigrant who is committed to stay may be shrugged off as just another incident by the student.

In the immigrant settlements in which the students of the Leadership Institute (the subjects of an earlier study) worked as teachers and counselors the food was often not to their taste and the accommodation frequently of a primitive kind; it is unlikely that they would have reconciled themselves to such conditions of existence for any lengthy period. But they did so uncomplainingly and indeed zestfully, for not only was the work among the immigrants seen by them as a significant task but as an adventure lasting a month only.

Social contact, too, is influenced, as we have seen, by the realization on the part of both the visitors and the hosts of the ephemeral nature of any relationship they establish. A few of the students during the year decided to remain in Israel, and it was noticeable how intent they became on establishing closer contact with Israelis. So one of them observed:

Once my decision was made, my approach to the life around me changed . . . I now felt myself to be a member of the Israeli society as a simple resident, a student at the University. I drew closer to other students who were also remaining; I began to meet and have something in common with Israeli students, and I drew even further away from the other students on my program.

When students at the Leadership Institute were asked what was the significance for them of a work period they spent in the kibbutzim, the prospective settlers among them checked "a test of the suitability of kibbutz life for me," whereas the nonsettlers gave priority of choice to "a chance to witness an interesting social experiment." Although the nonsettlers were critical of the "lack of privacy" and other stresses and strains in the life of the kibbutz, they were not seriously disturbed by what was for them an experience of limited duration, "as at a summer camp," one of them put it. On the other hand, those who intended to settle—more particularly those who belonged to youth movements advocating settlement in a kibbutz— were in a higher state of tension as they saw in the work period a crucial test of their capacity to adapt to a way of life they had tentatively chosen.

The students were aware that experiences undergone in the light of a particular time perspective were not always a safe guide to their ability to adjust permanently to one or another form of life in Israel. "I can say that 'if' I should come back I would just go to a kibbutz to see if I could take it as a 'kibbutznik' [a member of the kibbutz] and not a 'machonik' [member of the Institute] for a period of time."

During the fourth and final "pre-departure" phase the student is more than ever looking at his experiences in terms of their relevance to the back home period. He becomes increasingly aware of the impending need to resume relationships temporarily severed by his departure; the home reference groups gain in salience. But the thought of how he will be accepted on his return and to whom he will recount his experiences has in fact been present throughout the sojourn. The diary entries frequently indicate that when the student was undergoing some new experience he was thinking of how he would describe it to the "folks back home."

Not only was I seeing things which were fascinating and exciting, but I also saw things which will provide great material for lectures when I'm home.

Considering my feelings of Israel so far I wonder how and in what way I will be able to talk to people and Judaeans [members of Young Judaea organization] about Israel.

My roommate for this year with whom I was touring joined me in an unspoken agreement that the objective was as follows: To do as much travelling as possible in the two months we had before school began in order to see as many of the necessary places as possible (necessary being defined as the sort of spot that one could not admit having missed when returning from a year in Israel).

As the day of return approaches, the salience of home increases. At classes in the Leadership Institute in Jerusalem during the final month, the interest of the students could be aroused most strongly when the discussion concerned the problems awaiting them in the United States.

The students who have some foreknowledge of what awaits them on their return are in an advantageous position. Not only can they adjust their training more adequately to the likely needs, but the structured time perspective makes their morale higher than that of their fellows who are in the dark about their future back home.

The thought that they would soon be returning home allowed the students to postpone making decisions on several problems. Interviewed about their attitudes to a number of issues, some replied that they "would make up their minds when home," where supposedly they would be free from the constant pressure of new impressions. If the students had not felt it possible to postpone taking a stand, a greater measure of organization of the cognitive structure conceivably would have taken place at an earlier stage, that is *during* the sojourn.

On the other hand, the limited time perspective created

considerable impatience over other issues, such as sightseeing and contact with hosts. The awareness of the fleeting nature of the occasions for observation and interaction made the students anxious not to miss whatever opportunities occurred. They were accordingly fretful if for any reason an excursion into the country was canceled or if they failed to attend a festive celebration in which they were interested.

The responses of the students to the question of how they had felt during the various periods of their sojourn (the first two weeks, the rest of the ulpan period, the first two weeks of the university term, the remainder of the stay) reflected the alternation of moods characteristic of the different phases. Morale was high during the first two weeks but later declined. A new time sequence breaking the tedium began with the opening of the university term. A rise in spirits might have been anticipated at this stage, but difficulties in adjusting to the curriculum of studies apparently offset this rise. As the students settled down to their studies, the mood improved.[3] The alternating moods as the sojourn progressed can be diagrammatically represented in the form of a U-curve (Table 21). The measure of satisfaction a student feels about his sojourn will depend— to some extent, at any rate—on the point on the adjustment curve at which his mood stands when the sojourn is terminated.

Seeing the Country in Historical Time Perspective

If the students had viewed Israel merely as it appeared at the given moment in time corresponding to their arrival, their appraisal would in all probablility have been very different from what it was. Their perception of Israel was determined by a historical time perspective,[4] more clearly elaborated in the minds of some than of others, but operative in some measure for the great majority. They saw it as the land of the Bible, as a country which remained the Jewish homeland despite the dispersion of the Jewish people, as an old-new land being reclaimed after centuries of neglect.

The link which the Jewish people in all parts of the world have maintained through the centuries with the Land of Israel is one of the peculiar phenomena of history. The attitudes of the students reflected this deeply emotional relationship to the land. As one student remarked: "Israel is part of me and has been ever since I can remember." And another added: "I had to love Israel even before I saw it; I was just brought up that way."

The attachment of the students was primarily to Israel rather than to Israelis. They would more readily criticize Israelis than Israel for whatever they found amiss (although they had a feeling of closeness to Israelis whenever they saw them in their role of fellow-Jews). At times —as when they were irritated by excessive "red tape"—some of them even tended to differentiate between the State of Israel and the Land of Israel. One student drew this distinction very sharply: "There's always the Land which is why I am here in the first place—not because of the State. The State is not doing enough; it isn't living up to the promise of the Land. The Government is a bad thing for this country . . . also the bitter political bickering."

To the extent that the students were acquainted with the history of the Jewish people and of Israel, they were able to evaluate the country's achievements as well as to make allowance for its shortcomings. They would frequently temper their indignation about the inefficiency of a particular Israeli institution by observing that, after all, this was still a young state founded under difficult circumstances. Again, their admiration at an achievement would be enhanced by the reflection that all this had been accomplished within a few years. "My Yeshivah training and the Zionist tradition of my home enabled me to see Israel in more than a superficial light. It helps one round out the rough spots, filling things with sentimentality."

As the students saw it, the State of Israel represented the culmination of centuries of yearning for the Land of Israel. They viewed its establishment against the background of Jewish suffering, in particular the tragedy of European Jewry. Speaking of the bond between the Jews of the United States and of Israel, a student remarked: "In addition to the common history and culture, there's an association because of suffering, particularly World War II."

When asked to choose two from a list of five reasons justifying the existence of a State of Israel, the majority chose the longings of Jews in the Diaspora and their sufferings, rather than the achievements within Israel itself (Table 22). Such historic perspective provides a framework within which their own relationship as Jews to Israel finds its place.

Of interest is a comparison with Israeli high-school students to whom the same question was presented.[5] The Israelis ranked as most important "the suffering of Jews in the Diaspora," but followed this by the achievements within Israel ("the resettlement of the country in recent times and the War of Liberation"). "The recognition by the nations of the world of the idea of a Jewish state" is given more weight by the American students than by the Israelis, who place it lowest on the list (Table 23).

Historical Time Perspective and Involvement

The relationship of the students as Jews to Israel—their involvement in the country—can be adequately understood only in terms of this historical time perspective linking the country with the Jewish people.[6] They are hardly ever dispassionate about Israel. There is from the very outset of their stay an emotional tone to their reactions to the country and its people which would be unusual in other sojourners in a foreign country but is comprehensible in these students. Thus, a student, speaking heatedly about the problems of the Oriental communities in Israel and about inefficiency in Israeli administration, suddenly stops and asks herself why she is criticizing in this vein: "Maybe it is because I identify more here with Israel that I care more. In America I see myself as just another person. But here it is a Jewish state and a Jewish people, I can't say it is just humanity. It is a Jewish failure."

So too were the students deeply disconcerted whenever they met an Israeli who contemplated emigration from Israel to the United States: "I can't stand it if I see an Israeli who wants to settle in America. You feel that you have failed, that Israel has failed."

As the involvement grew, what they expressed resembled more the concern of someone on the inside and less the carping criticism or annoyance of the outsider. Contrasting her attitudes at different stages of the sojourn, a student, whose involvement, considerable at the outset, had further increased, remarked:

I was disappointed in the religious life—the attitude of non-religious to religious, of religious to non-religious . . . the tension I felt. I was in a battlefield in which I did not want to be. Now I've a better picture. Now it is just an unhappy fact. Over the months I've come to feel more part of it. It's different from a disappointment. There's a battlefield and I feel part of it.

In some cases the involvement produced a sense of responsibility to help change the face of things. A student who contemplated settlement in Israel observed:

There's nothing unfavorable to the extent that it would prevent me from coming back. At the same time I dislike the unawareness of Jewish feeling. It's not a point that angers me so much that it would make Israel or Israelis black. At the same time it angers me to the extent that something should be done. If I come to Israel I should want to teach. My feelings about the things I have mentioned would influence my teaching.

CHAPTER 9

The Intention to Settle:
The "Push" and the "Pull"

The students were linked with many ties to the country in which they had grown up. Their families and friends lived in the States. Their training had been based on the assumption of a continued residence there, and the way to a career and secure livelihood appeared to be open. The United States is not a country of emigration. Why should they have been disposed to give even the slightest thought to settlement elsewhere? They were, of course, not just students visiting a foreign land; they were Jews and the country was Israel (and it was clear that they would not think of leaving the United States for any place other than Israel). But is necessary to go beyond this statement and to explore the convergence of motivational factors which disposed these American Jewish students to consider transplanting their lives to Israel.

Whenever they discussed settling in Israel, the students were at pains to emphasize that they were considering such a possibility because of the positive attraction, the "pull" of Israel, not because of any "push" from America. The prevailing norm in the groups to which they belonged was to speak of *aliyah* (immigration to Israel) in this manner. Particularly insistent about this were the students who had declared an intention of settling, even though they viewed the

potential danger of antisemitism in the United States somewhat more seriously than the others. Persons approaching a
goal tend indeed to think largely in terms of the drawing-
power of such a goal and often forget that somewhere
along the line a "push" existed.[1]

The ties which bound the students to America were
strong, and it is not to be supposed that the attraction of Israel could *in itself* have sufficed to break them. Did the students then feel any sense of discomfiture or unease about
their position in America which made them contemplate so
radical a decision as that of settling in another country?[2]
We need to examine the nature and the source of such
"push" as may have existed.

Antisemitism and the Memory of the Holocaust

For the students, the "push" was not a direct reaction to
the grosser manifestations of antisemitism. Although they
were not oblivious of the existence of antisemitism, the majority did not regard it as a potentially serious threat
(Table 24). Students hailing from New York and other cities with large Jewish populations found difficulty in recall-
ing antisemitic incidents in which they were personally involved. When asked to choose among courses of action
important for an American Jewish community, "fight antisemitism" received relatively little support; it was chosen
by only 10 per cent of the students (Table 55). Indeed
overt antisemitism apparently decreased during the two
decades which constituted the life-span of the students, and
in 1965 it did not seem to be prominent in the consciousness of American Jews.[3]

A comparison of their attitudes with those of a group of
American Jewish students of similar background studied in

1946 reveals a difference in this respect.[4] The students of that period had been deeply moved by the destruction of European Jewry. They viewed any manifestation of antisemitism as serious because they saw it against the background of the events in Europe. In 1965 students no longer saw antisemitism within that wider context. When references to the tragedy of European Jewry did occur, the students tended to disclaim rather than affirm a connection between events in Europe and the situation in America.

In Israel the students heard dire prophecies from their hosts—who often drew an analogy with what had happened in Europe—about the spread of antisemitism in the United States. They treated those warnings with disdain. The warnings, moreover, were almost invariably associated with criticism of the reluctance of American Jews to immigrate to Israel, and criticism in this form generally evoked defensive reactions on the part of the students.

The disclaimers of a connection between antisemitism in America and the Holocaust in Europe did not mean, however, that this vast tragedy did not affect the thinking of the students. It was no longer salient, but the question was whether there were traces of its influence in the recesses of their minds. Although they belonged to a generation born after the Holocaust they had been reminded of it only a few years previously by the Eichmann trial. From the detailed, focused interviews, the impression emerged that the thought of the Holocaust simmered at the back of their minds. Occasionally the thought came to the surface, as when a student commented:

Since World War II I think Jews the world over have been instilled with a doubt as to their safety in any country under any government. A lot of confidence in the humanity of the non-Jewish world has been lost. For this reason many Jews see

Israel as a place where they can be sure no antisemitism will arise.

During their sojourn they were frequently reminded of the Holocaust. They reported with compassion on meetings with concentration camp survivors with numbers tattooed on their arms; they were present at Remembrance Day ceremonies (in memory of martyred European Jewry); issues regarding relations between Israel and West Germany were given headlines in the press during this period. When the students were asked, "Has the Holocaust (the destruction of European Jewry) influenced your thinking on Jewish life?" 84 per cent answered in the affirmative (Table 25). Although the memory of the Holocaust constituted a background situation subtly influencing even a generation born after World War II and interpenetrating many of its attitudes, the interviews indicated that the unease of the students stemmed more directly from one or more sources related to their Jewish identity in a non-Jewish environment.[5]

Sources of Unease

1. As the importance of the Jewish strand in their identity grew, the discontent of some of the students increased over the impingement of the pervasive majority culture on the full, undiluted expression of their Jewishness and over the compromises they were called upon to make when the values or practices of the majority and minority were not fully consonant. The more important a student's Jewishness was to him, the more likely he was to be concerned about the concessions the minority is called upon to make to the majority culture. So a religious student remarked after arrival in Israel: "Here in Israel I am found constantly

with a 'kipah' [skull-cap] on my head . . . Israel society accepts the man with his head covered. In the States one doesn't feel comfortable or secure. Being different is not always condoned by American society."

Another student with an intense Jewish identification observed: "American culture may be secular but it is secular in a Christian way. The framework in the U.S. is Christian and this framework is the basic thing you relate back to. Here (in Israel) the culture is secular in a Jewish way."

2. There was an awareness that the majority did not accept them at all points. While the students agreed that the cruder forms of antisemitism were not much in evidence, they at times had sensed a more subtle, less tangible, form of hostility. Even if they personally had not suffered from it, they were nevertheless not oblivious of the fact that Jews are excluded from, or are unwelcome in, certain spheres. The more sensitive the student, the more likely he was to resent a situation of this kind even though he was not necessarily anxious about it. One student declared:

I never felt any definite outright antisemitism. I never saw any demonstrations of it. But there certainly is an uncomfortable feeling of some sort on which you cannot put your finger. I could almost feel it between my roommate and myself. It was as if he was saying "I like you in spite of the fact that you are Jewish"—although he would never actually say it.

A positive, though not very high, measure of association exists between intention to settle and a serious view of the threat antisemitism constitutes.[6]

3. Some of the students who were not religiously observant but wished to identify with their Jewish group had difficulty in finding form and content for their Jewishness in

the United States. In a sense they were engaged in a search for a meaningful secular Jewish identity. One student spoke of Israel as the "best place to feel Jewish without being religious." A nonreligious student with strong Jewish identification observed:

Most Jews, especially in America, can't find something in religion. They feel a need for some kind of substitute to express themselves Jewishly. In "Chutz la'aretz" you have to find all kinds of ideologies, things to hang onto. But it doesn't really solve the problem. Once you live here (in Israel) most of the questions don't arise and there is not so much need for ideology.

A Jew may view and react in various ways to these three sources of discomfiture. But, if he sees them as inherent in the American environment and not in another environment provided by a Jewish majority, that other environment will gain in attractiveness for him. Each of our students in his own way, whether he intended to settle or not, hoped to find in Israel what he lacked as a Jew in America. Some turned to it as an environment in which the discord between Jewish values and others did not exist, where they could live a fully Jewish life; others saw in it a society where a Jew "belonged" and the problem of acceptance did not arise; still others viewed it as a place where they did not have to strain to find a specifically religious expression to their Jewish identity.

The "Jewish" Satisfactions

The experience of the sojourn confirmed and strengthened the favorable feelings the students had about Israel before they came to the country. But Israel's main drawing-power lay in the fact that it seemed to provide an answer to the problems of Jewish identity inherent in a non-Jewish environment. When asked what most attracted them personally about life in Israel, the majority of the students checked the three "Jewish" alternatives. "I could feel at home here as a Jew" came first, followed by "I could enjoy a more complete Jewish cultural life" and "I could live a completely Jewish religious life here" (Table 26).

The "push" and "pull" were really two sides of the same coin. The satisfactions peculiar to Israel were those which could not be obtained by the students qua Jews in the United States, in other words, "Jewish" satisfactions. The following are typical of the replies to the question "What satisfactions do you think you may get from life in Israel which you cannot get in America?"

The satisfaction of living in a country which is *mine*—the satisfaction of feeling an undisturbed unity with the rest of the population.

In Israel I feel a Jewish fulfilment while in America I feel a Jewish self-consciousness.

There was a significant relationship between position on the Jewish–American continuum and intention to settle; i.e., the closer a student was to the Jewish end of the continuum, the more likely he was to consider settlement.[7]

Among the different religious categories (Orthodox, Conservative, Reform and Nonreligious) the Orthodox students had the most positive inclination towards settlement (Table 27). But a cautionary note should be sounded. Just as the students who visit Israel cannot be regarded as representative of American Jewish students as a whole, so those who belonged to the religious subgroups were not necessarily representative of those subgroups.

When the students themselves (in this case the 1966 group) were asked which category of Jews was most likely to have a desire to settle in Israel, the Orthodox Jews were accorded first place. Even those students who themselves were not Orthodox accorded Orthodox Jews this preference (Table 28). Typical of the explanations was this response: "Orthodox Jews see settling in Israel a mitzvah [religious obligation]. Also it is easier here to observe the mitzvot [religious obligations], the ideal place to bring up children in a religious surrounding." At the same time a minority of the students felt that the nonreligious may be most inclined to settle. They explained that those secular Jews who are anxious to preserve their ties with the Jewish people may wish to live in a society where religious observance is not the primary criterion of Jewish affiliation. "If they feel a strong national tie they are free to develop these feelings here. They may feel at home here because most of the Israelis are non-religious, yet they are still Jews."

The Paths to a Decision

We have outlined the background factors which motivated the students to visit Israel and in some cases to think seriously of settling in the country. But this analysis does not tell us *how* the students were influenced in this direction and how motivation becomes linked with action. For an adequate account of the steps in a student's progression toward a decision, we would need to look at the stages through which he passed prior to his arrival in Israel. The material gathered in the present study, however, related mainly to the influence of the *sojourn* in Israel, and did not allow for a proper assessment of the earlier formative influences such as home, Jewish education, summer camps, or youth organizations.

In tracing the path to a decision, a comparison may be useful between students in the American Student Program at the Hebrew University and one of the groups we studied previously at the Institute for Youth Leaders from Abroad. We shall first discuss the Institute group, and will then turn to the students of our present study.

Decision Process at the Leadership Institute

A distinction has to be drawn between two categories of students at the Institute in terms of their initial attitudes on their arrival. Twenty-seven of the fifty-eight students arrived with a declared intention to settle—not in the immediate future, but after the completion of the two years service they had promised to render to their movements on their return from Israel. They were known as the *chalutzim* (a term usually reserved for pioneers who have actually settled on the land). The remaining thirty-one were, by contrast, referred to as *nonchalutzim*.

The chalutzim belonged to Zionist youth movements which stressed pioneering in Israel. Our interviews showed that when they had been first approached to join the groups, they had little or no knowledge of their ideology —in fact, some of them were young children when they enrolled. As they became involved in the life of the group, they gradually accepted its norms and had reached the point of declaring an intention to settle.

This intention was not always firm. The fact that it related to life in a country they had never seen, and that they could not realistically weigh all the considerations at a distance, had given it a tentative character. For most of them, therefore, the visit to Israel was a voyage of exploration to determine whether they would eventually be able to fit into Israeli life. Even though in the case of the majority the intention to settle was maintained and strengthened (Table 29), the students nonetheless experienced much heart-searching when testing the "decision" against reality, whether in the kibbutzim or in the towns.

For the nonchalutzim the progression toward a decision was understandably slow. That such a decision became at all feasible (Table 29) was due to the combination of "push" and "pull" referred to earlier, and to the fact that the stranger group fostered pro-aliyah norms. On this score, the chalutzim set the tone at the Institute, and just as they had reached their intention within the social climate of their movements in the United States, so the stranger group now provided the context in which the nonchalutzim could find the necessary stimulation and support.

No student could remain impervious to the question of whether or not he would settle; indeed it became one of the salient issues of their sojourn. The Israelis who saw them as eligible and desirable—albeit not very likely—candidates for settlement would invariably challenge them with a question of this kind. Inside the stranger group the subject was frequently discussed. (When asked to describe the significance of the stay in Israel, 70 per cent of the students checked as one of the chosen alternatives that it had provided "an opportunity to know Israel better with my possible aliya in view.") Although there were barriers in the way of a decision, they were not as serious for a student still in the stage of exploring occupational choices [8] as for an older person with fixed commitments.

Despite the favorable social climate and the pressures to which they were subjected, the progression toward a decision of such far-reaching consequence was always gradual.[9] Thus the students were asked, "Do you intend to settle in Israel?" before their departure from the United States, at the end of five months in Jerusalem, at the end of the year in Israel, and again on their return to America. The list of responses ranged from "no" through "uncertain and unlikely," "uncertain but possibly," "uncertain but likely" to "yes." Throughout the year the progression of the students along the ladder of responses was rarely more than one rung at a time (Table 30).

The change in attitudes produced by the experiences of the sojourn was gradual, and only when this change had advanced to a certain point were the students psychologically ready to make a decision. The decision was indeed the culmination of a development which began far back in the United States, in the home, the Hebrew school, or youth organization. It reflected a new balance of forces. In response to the question of why she intended to settle a student replied: "I can't answer. Just feel it without being able to explain. I feel myself more a part of Israel. I feel myself more a Jew than an American. . . . It's unnatural to be a Jew in the States. I have to be forcing it."

By the end of the year, however, the majority of students indicated not a final *decision* but rather an *intention* [10]—a heightened motivation—to settle. A decision implies that there no longer is vacillation, that whatever counter-arguments or contrary considerations existed have been definitely dismissed. But our analysis of the students' development shows that while during the year the psychological forces in favor of settlement arising out of the growing attraction of Israel mounted in strength, certain considerations against settlement continued to operate unabated. Such considerations were the opposition of parents, the reluctance of students to uproot themselves, the need for further training in the United States. The increase in what may be termed "driving forces" [11] without a decrease in "opposing" or "restraining forces" resulted in high tension and in a deferment of the decision. A student caught in this conflict wrote in his diary:

The difficult part of my decision for or against aliya is that neither decision is really clearcut, nor do I see that it can ever be. It just isn't a matter of black or white. There are too many incomplete, unclear and uncertain conclusions that will have to be made . . . I must admit that I am afraid to make a determined conclusion.

Decision in the A.S.P.

When they came to Israel, only a few of the students (4 per cent) in the 1965 American Student Program had a clear intention to settle although many of the others did not rule out such a possibility.

The majority regarded settlement in Israel as irrelevant to the question of whether a Jew in America could be considered a "good Jew." This contrasted with the view of Israeli high school students, who placed such requirement high on the list of characteristics of a "good Jew" abroad (Table 31).

The students were frequently challenged by Israelis about their intention to settle. They were at times irritated at the way the demand was presented without due consideration of the difficulties. "I don't think they are completely open to listening to the problems of American Jewry. They feel that everybody should come here as a Jew." And another student, who wishes to settle but hesitates to sever the ties with family and friends, feels that the painful conflict she faces is too lightly dismissed by Israelis. "Most of them don't try to understand what it means to leave and come. They think it is so easy to pack your bags." The challenge could not, however, be ignored and the subject was frequently discussed among the students. "Most people are beginning to ask themselves whether they are coming on aliyah or not. This is becoming more and more a topic of conversation."

During the final months of their stay some of the students took the initiative in calling together from time to time fellow-students who were interested in clarifying for themselves the possibility of settlement. In these discussions the difficulties in the path of the would-be settler were considered as well as the reasons why the step was desirable. Since they were all students, mostly in their junior year, intent upon completing their studies, they felt that no immediate decision was warranted. There was no group with a clearly defined pro-settlement norm (such as had existed at the Institute) which could serve as a source of reference to those pondering the issue.

Toward the end of the sojourn only limited changes had taken place in their attitudes (Table 32). As with the students at the Institute, the changes that did take place were principally of one rung in the ladder. In a few cases the changes were of two rungs; in no case was there a change of three or four rungs (Table 33).

When interviewed at the end of the year, the majority were still weighing the pros and cons of personal aliyah; only a minority expressed a clear intention one way or the other. A question about the relative disadvantages of being a Jew in the United States and being an American in Israel elicited a diversity of responses. For some students, unable to gain acceptance by Israelis or impressed by the difficulties of adjusting to a culture other than that in which they had been socialized, the disadvantages of being an American in Israel were salient; these were generally students who were not inclined to settle in Israel.

The American is not completely used to Israeli culture, which he did not grow up in. Too, Israelis at some levels are prejudiced against foreigners.

The Jew in America has almost no disadvantage to speak of, he can live a Jewish life in America. An American must change a way of life to adapt to Israel.

I feel an integral part of American society, while I still feel a member of an outgroup here.

Others regarded their being Americans in Israel as the more tolerable disadvantage. They hoped that this disadvantage could be minimized with increasing adjustment to Israeli society, whereas they felt that whatever disadvantage attached to their position as Jews in American society would remain unchanged with the passage of time. These were students inclined to consider settlement in Israel.

The problem in Israel can be eventually solved in a matter of time and adaptation. In the U.S. the problem will not be resolved. It is a large social and cultural problem that the individual cannot change.

The Jew in the U.S. doesn't "belong" quite as much as he does here in Israel.

To me my Jewishness is more important than my being an American. I am thankful that I lived in America but it isn't the place for Jews.

And another student, who had already taken a decision not to return to the States but to continue her studies in Jerusalem, summed up her views with the conviction of someone no longer beset by doubts: "What is important for me is to be a Jew in Israel."

CHAPTER 10

Effects of the Sojourn

A year's sojourn by students in a foreign country, in a total environment sharply different from the culture in which they have been socialized, is bound to produce changes beyond those that would occur in the ordinary course of maturation. In delineating the psychological field of the foreign student we mapped out what seemed to us the contexts in which these changes in cognition, in values, and in action occur.[1]

For many students the changes may not be fundamental. What has been achieved through years of socialization, particularly in the realm of values, cannot readily be undone—not even in the malleable young. This held true also for our students, but not to quite the same extent. As a result of their peculiar involvement as Jews in the host society of Israel they were subject to value changes of a kind not generally undergone by foreign students.[2]

The Nature of the Changes

We would expect changes to take place more readily on the action level. The foreign student is obliged to conform to certain of the behavioral requirements of the host society. As a result there may be changes in matters such as dress and food habits. At the same time these are merely temporary, expedient adjustments to the demands of the immediate environment; there is no need to retain them and they generally are not retained on the return home. But our students differ in this respect too, for they were called upon to consider action changes of a far-reaching character extending beyond the period of the sojourn, such as increased activity in Jewish organizations and the eventual permanent transplantation of their lives to Israel.

The changes that do occur as the result of a sojourn in a foreign country are mostly on the cognitive level. Although some stereotypes about the host country and hosts persist, change does take place not only in the way the host-country is perceived but also in the picture of the home country. At a number of points the country of sojourn comes to serve as a source of comparative reference, thus giving the students a different perspective on various facets of the home environment. This was particularly so in our study where the prior emotional attachment of the students to Israel made them more readily accept this country as a source of reference.

We have earlier discussed how the salience of a given situation influences the ethnic role assumed by the students. Our study suggests that salience is equally a key concept in the analysis of changes in the cognitive structure; a study of cross-cultural education must take into account the effect of the changing salience of features of the host country, once viewed from afar and now experienced at first-hand.

The psychological regions corresponding to activities in the host society as perceived by the students are (or become) differentiated into subregions. The region of "life in a collective settlement" includes subregions such as "life of equality," "privacy," "agricultural work." Each of these subregions has a valence of its own—"life of equality" may be evaluated positively, whereas "agricultural work" may be evaluated negatively. The total valence of the region is then determined by the valences and *saliences* of the subregions: the higher the salience of a subregion, the greater the weight of its valence in determining the valence of the total region.

The changes in the salience of the subregions will usually not be uniform; some subregions will gain or lose more in salience than will others. Thus, even if the valence of each subregion remains constant, the valence of the total region changes, and a perceptual process brings about a change in evaluations.

This process was strikingly exemplified in our earlier study at the Institute by the changes in attitude to life in a kibbutz. There were some students who after spending a period in a kibbutz looked upon this form of settlement with less favor than before their coming. Their support of the communal ideology remained unaffected, they still found the security offered by the kibbutz attractive, but what happened was that another of the subregions, most frequently the "lack of privacy," of which they may have known abstractly before and even then viewed with disfavor, assumed heightened salience in the light of their own experience of life in the kibbutz. "I never really thought about it" was a characteristic remark about such subregions, whose valence—positive or negative—remained constant, but which now gained strongly in salience and hence produced a change in the evaluation of the region as a whole.

We have discussed the *nature* of the changes. Three sets of interrelated factors determine their *direction*. First are the initial attitudes of the students which influence their selection and interpretation of the elements in their new experience. Our students came with highly favorable dispositions towards the host country. Second is the satisfaction or otherwise with the experiences in the host society. The students expressed general satisfaction with the sojourn except in certain spheres (difficulties in social contact with Israelis, lack of rapport on some problems, irritation with administrative inefficiency). Finally, there is the reference (or absence of it) to groups in the new environment. In our study the stranger group was a frequent source of reference, and its norms played a considerable part in determining attitudes to the host country and to various aspects of the sojourn.

We shall proceed to discuss changes in the students which occurred in three areas: in their perception of the bases of alignment among Jews in general as well as, more specifically, between Israelis and American Jews, in their evaluation of Israel and Israelis, and in their self-identity.

Perception of the Bases of Alignment

The students brought with them a sense of close kinship with Jews everywhere. The feelings of kinship remained strong when put to the test of a meeting with the many different types of Jews in Israel; the slight downward trend was not statistically significant (Table 34). The question remains whether this encounter produced any change in their perception of the basis of alignment between themselves and other Jews.

On their way to Israel the students were asked about the extent of the similarity they perceived among Jews in "culture and customs," "characteristics and behavior," and "appearance." At that time 72 per cent of the students regarded Jews as either "very similar" or "similar" in "culture and customs"; a lesser percentage (48 per cent) found such similarity in regard to "characteristics and behavior," and still fewer (11 per cent) saw similarity in "appearance." The meeting in Israel with so variegated an assortment of Jews, drawn from East as well as West, reduced the sense of similarity on all three scores (Tables 35, 36, and 37).

A further set of identical questions related to the similarity "between Israelis and American Jews." A comparison between the responses of the students to the two sets of questions on board ship shows that more of them expected some degree of difference "between Israelis and American Jews" (when thus placed in juxtaposition) than "among Jews" in both "culture and customs" and "characteristics and behavior," though not in "appearance" (Table 38).

After the students had met the Israelis, their position remained unchanged about the difference between Israelis and American Jews in the realm of "culture and customs" (Table 39). But this was apparently an overall view, and their prior cognition of dissimilarities did not temper the chagrin a number of them experienced, as the interviews reveal, when in the specific area of religious observance they came into contact with practices different from what they were accustomed to in America.

There was also no significant change on the score of "characteristics and behavior," although there was a slight tendency to record less of a difference (Table 40). Qualifications need, however, to be introduced when we examine their evaluation of specific characteristics (on the Semantic Differential administered on the two occasions). Whereas for a few characteristics, such as "materialistic-idealistic," the difference between Israeli and American Jew had contracted, on others, such as "sociability" and "courtesy," the gap had widened considerably.

It was in regard to the "appearance" of Israelis that the sense of difference decreased markedly. The similarity now seen by the students "between Israelis and American Jews" was considerably greater than that perceived by them "among Jews." Under the impact of the experiences of the sojourn, only 15 per cent of the students still recognized any appreciable similarity ("very similar" or "similar") among Jews in appearance, but 41 per cent now found such similarity between Israelis and American Jews (Tables 37 and 41).

The interviews indicate that the term "Israelis" conjured up for many of the students the picture of sabras, especially the Israeli students they had met on the campus or the members of kibbutzim they had visited. These Israelis, though dissimilar in other respects, were not so different in *appearance* from American Jews as were many of the immigrants, more particularly those from countries of the Orient.

Similarity and Interdependence

The interviews and diaries indicate that the basis provided by the feeling of similarity for alignment among Jews (or between Israelis and American Jews) was even more limited and tenuous than the questionnaire responses would imply. After walking through the streets of Jerusalem one bewildered student wrote: "Before I came to Israel I thought all Jews were one people. I am not so sure now."

Kurt Lewin has pointed out the importance of viewing group belongingness as based on interdependence rather than on similarity.[3] Within the Jewish group, as in others, there are great variations of outlook and custom as well as other dissimilarities. What is important, however, as the main criterion of belongingness is interdependence.

The dissimilarities the students encountered were obtru-

sive, and their thinking about their relationship to other
Jews or to Israelis was often in terms of similarity or dissimilarity: "I find it difficult to identify with non-Ashkena-
zim." "I cannot regard Jews like the Falashas or the Cochin
Jews as kith and kin but European Jews I do regard."

When they had occasion, however, to think in terms of interdependence their belongingness in common to a Jewish
group became manifest. "I feel we need to stick together,
especially today (we Jews—that is)." "What happens to
them (though many of us are different) affects me in some
way, and vice versa."

The students were more ready to regard Jews as interdependent rather than as similar, and their position on this
subject remained virtually unchanged through the year.
They were particularly responsive to situations where Jews
were under attack. Thus, 91 per cent either "always" or
"often" felt personally insulted when there was an insult
against the Jewish people (Table 43). The majority felt
that their fate and future were bound up with the fate and
future of the Jewish people (Table 44). A significant relationship exists between the sense of common fate expressed
in the response on this question and the location of the students on the Jewish side of the Jewish-American scale.[4]

The students recognized that the interdependence exists
not only between the individual Jew and the Jewish people
but also among Jewish communities. A decline in the prestige of the State of Israel was seen as affecting the American Jewish community, and vice versa (Tables 45 and 46).

Related to the feeling of interdependence is a sense of
mutual responsibility.[5] The great majority of students
brought with them, and maintained, an appreciation of the
reciprocal responsibilities of the two communities—Israel

and American Jewry. At the same time the responsibility
of American Jewry to Israel was seen as the greater (Tables 47 and 48).

Evaluation of Israel and Israelis

The highly favorable attitude toward Israel the students
brought with them was maintained through the year. Their
perception of Israel, the State, became more realistic, but
apparently the change in perception did not affect their attitude, which was anchored in their deep attachment to the
"Land of Israel." A student drew a distinction between the
two conceptions of Israel:

My view of Israel, that is, the land, in the holy, almost mysti-
cal sense of "the Land of Israel" has not changed at all. This
view was implanted in my mind when I was very young, and
neither my being in Israel, nor my being away from it, have
altered it. Actually, it is more an emotional than a rational
view. My view of Israel, as a political entity, a developing nation state, has changed.

At the same time in her subsequent description of her
"very favorable" attitude she made no differentiation between the two.

Although the idealized image of Israel was impaired
somewhat by the reality the students encountered, they
nonetheless felt more intimately linked to the country at
the end of the sojourn and most of them accepted it for
what it is. A student insightfully analyzed her feelings:

I am at this point much more critical and yet more tolerant
of Israel and her faults. It is as though the country has become more and more my own, more of a reality and less of
a dream. I am more critical in that I am aware of and very unhappy about much of what is wrong with the country. I am

more tolerant in that it makes me love it none the less. I think
that when I arrived I loved the country for what it represented, and thought that was the end of it. Now I find that I
actually love the country for what it is. That's the closest I can
come to expressing the sense of belonging that I now possess.

The students also came to Israel with a favorable image
of the "Israeli," more favorable than the image they had of
either the "American Jew" or "American non-Jew." Thus,
when the Semantic Differential was administered to the students as part of the questionnaire they completed on board
the ship, they rated the Israelis more highly [6] than they did
the other two groups (Tables 49 and 50).

The Pre-arrival Image of the "Israeli"

The Israeli was seen by the students as invested in particular with virtues associated with the new type of self-reliant Jew. He stood considerably ahead of the American
Jew and the American non-Jew on adjectives such as
"strong," "man of deeds," "free," "idealistic," and "self-respecting"; he was credited with greater "pride in his Jewishness" and "roots in his Jewishness" than the American
Jew; he was seen as abundantly "proud of being an Israeli."
The idyllic image had already been impaired somewhat
in the United States by what the students had heard about
the Israeli's lack of the social graces. In respect to these
qualities the Israeli was viewed in a less favorable light even
before the students reached the shores of Israel. He was
rated as less "sociable" than either the American Jew or
non-Jew, as less "courteous" than either. He was suspected
of being less "warm" than the American Jew, but yet
"warmer" than the American Jew's gentile neighbour. Similarly he was regarded as less "tolerant" than the American
Jew but more "tolerant" than the non-Jew. The students

rated their future hosts high on "hospitality"—on a par with the American Jew and non-Jew.

The Israeli and American Jew were in almost equal measure "clever" and "progressive," more so than the non-Jew. The American non-Jew rated highest on "religious," with American Jew and Israeli a poor second and third, respectively (Table 49).

The overall image of the Israeli, however, was favorable, and in the first days of their sojourn some of the students eagerly sought examples of Israelis who conformed to the picture they brought with them. "Her manner typified the type of Israeli I've been trying to find." "Very fine bunch of boys. I think they are the closest I've seen so far to what my ideal was of the Israeli youth before I came here."

A Decline in Favorableness

When the Semantic Differential was readministered in the second half of the sojourn (for the concepts "American Jew," "Israeli" and "myself as I am") the responses reflected some of the disillusionment which the students had suffered in their encounter with Israelis. There was a marked decline in the favorableness of the picture of the Israeli drawn by the students (Tables 50 and 51). The contact with the Israelis made manners a salient issue for the students. In reply to a question asked at the time they were on the ship, as to what was "not so good about Israel," 18 per cent of the students gave responses which could be categorized as relating to negative behavioral characteristics of Israelis, such as "arrogance" and "bad manners." When this question was repeated later during the sojourn itself, the responses of 58 per cent of the students fell into this category.

The decline occurred in all the adjectives in the Semantic

Differential except "hospitable," "proud of being an Israeli," and "self-respecting" (in regard to which the change is negligible). Particularly marked is the change in the ratings on "idealistic," "progressive," and "courteous" (the adjective on which the Israelis are rated lower than on any other on the list). Also significant statistically are the lower ratings on "sociable" and "warm"—reflections of the disappointment of the students in social contact with Israelis (Tables 51 and 52).

Although the extent of the difference decreased, "Israeli" still maintained a higher rating than "American Jew" on adjectives which may be considered as reflecting his status as a member of a Jewish majority society shaping its own destiny. These are the adjectives "strong," "man of deeds," "self-respecting," "free," "proud of being Jewish," and "having roots in Jewishness."

The students now saw the American Jew, in the light of the contrast provided by their Israeli hosts, as more "religious" than before (widening the gap between "Israeli" and "American Jew") and as less "materialistic" (almost closing the gap on this adjective between "Israeli" and "American Jew").

The decline in the favorableness of the Israeli stands out even more boldly when a comparison is made with the students' picture of themselves as reflected in the ratings of "myself as I am" (Table 53). Before their arrival in Israel the students rated the Israeli far ahead of themselves (one point and more) on "industrious," "strong," and "man of deeds." As against this, "myself" was considerably ahead (one point and more) on "honest," "tolerant," "courteous," and "religious." Later in the sojourn "myself" had a substantial lead also on "sociable," "pleasant," "progressive," "warm," "idealistic," "roots in Jewishness." While the Israeli's superiority as "industrious," "strong," and as "a man of deeds" was maintained, it was somewhat reduced in the minds of the students at the end of the months of contact. Before the students reached Israel the distance between "myself" and "Israeli" was less than that between "myself" and "American Jew." Toward the end of the sojourn "myself" was closer to "American Jew" than to "Israeli."

Within the limited universe encompassed by the adjectives on the Semantic Differential there was thus a clear decline in the favorableness of the picture of the Israeli (although the overall rating—4.74—cannot be said to be unfavorable). The question which needs to be examined is to what extent the tarnished image was accompanied by a change in attitude toward Israelis.

A Distinction between Israel and Israelis

Already prior to their arrival the students had differentiated between Israel and Israelis. Although the attitude to both was favorable, the attitude to Israel was the more so. While Israel maintained its high position in the esteem of the students, there was a slight decline, though not of significant size, in their regard for Israelis, widening the difference on this score between Israel and Israelis (Table 54). In the interviews a number of students drew the distinction between Israel and Israelis with considerable sharpness. "Whether Israelis make a good impression on me or not, Israel is still my home." Another student explained that "toward Israel I feel 'we'; toward Israelis 'they'." And one of the students, who intends to settle in Israel, went further and suggested that the future of Israel should not lie only in the hands of the native Israelis: "I see potential in Israel, and don't want to leave the potential lie undeveloped in Sabra hands."

Some of the aura of the land nonetheless carries over to its inhabitants and the distinction was not complete. Moreover, as the students stood in wonder before some of the achievements of modern Israel, they recognized that this was the handiwork of Israelis. One student put it this way: "Israel is not only the ruins of the past. It is an Israeli product. There is an identity." And another remarks: "The country itself has a driving force which inspires the people on."

This linkage between Israel and Israelis may account in part for the continued, though slightly diminished, favorableness of the students' attitude to Israelis despite the changes registered in the Semantic Differential. Indeed on the Semantic Differential the picture of the Israeli was least dimmed in respect to those qualities (such as "strong," "free," "self-respecting," "man of deeds," "proud of being an Israeli") with which he was seen as invested by virtue of his association with an independent and self-reliant Israel.

An ambivalence crept into the attitudes of the students toward Israelis. On the one hand they were taken aback by their lack of courtesy and by bureaucratic inefficiency; on the other hand they were impressed by the achievements and by the hospitality of the Israelis. Thus a student remarked:

The Israelis aren't perfect; they make mistakes. They certainly are bureaucratic and inefficient. But in general they are not so inefficient, things are done and that's what's important. . . . There's quite a bit of a mess. But they can't be inefficient after all they've accomplished.

It would seem that, although in the course of the contact with Israelis the "discourteous" and "unsociable" behavior so widely attributed to them caused the students considerable irritation and at times even anguish, they tended not to allow these objectionable characteristics to impair too markedly the otherwise favorable "gestalt." So a student who experienced a series of disconcerting encounters with Israeli "rudeness" was still hesitant in her criticism about them and remarked charitably: "I guess my view of Israelis remains a little uncertain—there is a gap between what I'd like to feel and what I saw and see."

Changes in Self-Identity

The sojourn in Israel represented for the students an experiment in Jewish living which had direct pertinence to their future way of life. The principal change indeed relates to so central an area as their self-identity.[7] The subtler nuances of this change are discernible in the interviews, letters, essays and diaries (rather than in the formal questionnaires).

During the year they were in a society in which "being Jewish" was not confined to specific, limited areas of life. "I appreciated being a 'full-time Jew' here (in Israel) and not just a Jew in my own life at home or in the Synagogue," a student remarked. They encountered new ways of Jewish living and expressions of Jewish identification which invited a different, and broader, conception of Jewishness than that they brought with them. They were continually comparing their Jewishness with that of the Israelis. Unlike other students in a foreign country for whom the habits of their hosts may be a subject of detached, fleeting interest, they were aware that the patterns of Jewish living practiced in the host society had a significance for them which could extend beyond the year of the sojourn.

Initially a good deal of confusion, and at times even dismay, prevailed at the unexpected complexities. After speaking enthusiastically about the modern expression of Judaism in Israel as "a free, natural, exuberant force . . . I feel part of it," a student remarked sadly: "There's also a perplexity on my part. Before I didn't know about the Eastern aspects of my Jewish background and the tremendous problem of the unity of the Jewish people."

In this situation in which they could no longer cling unquestioningly to the accustomed forms of American Jewish living, the students began to re-examine their own way of life—in essence what "being Jewish" meant to them. The visit of a number of the students to Israel was in fact part of a search for the Jewish meaning of their lives and they seized upon the opportunity the stay provided for clarifying the problem. A student, who was conscious of his attempt at such clarification, observed:

Israel offers the challenge to the Jew not only to live his Jewishness in every day-to-day experience, but also to strip himself of his Diaspora-bred pretensions and seek the sustenance of life on other than his own personal terms. This is difficult, but at least for me vital as an attempt. I do not think I would ever realize a real Jewish life without an Israel-based experience, and I believe that those who deprive themselves of it are not realistic about Jewish life.

In the States the expressions of "being Jewish" took a primarily religious form. In reviewing the sojourn the students frequently stressed that the year in Israel made it clear to them that this was too limited a conception. The following were typical remarks:

I now have a broader view of what "being Jewish" means which extends beyond religion though, personally, I find it difficult to envision myself identified as Jewish without religious attachments.

I got to understand the other parts of being a Jew while here. I can take it more naturally.

The very fact of their coming to Israel had been a reflection of the link between their Jewishness and Israel, but they now recognized more clearly that there could be no adequate definition of being Jewish in the contemporary world which did not take into account the relationship between Jewish identity and Israel.

Being Jewish means more than a commitment to religion and nation; today it must of necessity include a predominant commitment to Israel, for without it, one cannot really be "Jewish."

Being Jewish does involve some form of commitment to Israel, now, whereas before it didn't.

Decision and Identity

All the students were confronted squarely with the question whether they intended settling in Israel. It was treated by some with greater and by others with less seriousness. No one, however, could escape the need to formulate a response to a question posed not only by Israeli hosts but in time by their American fellow-students among whom it became a subject of frequent discussion. The challenge demanded some thought to their future geographical location —and all such location implied.

Sixty-two per cent of the students did not rule out settlement in Israel. Of this number, 11 per cent, as indicated earlier, expressed an unqualified intention, another 10 per cent felt they were "likely" to settle, and 41 per cent thought that they might "possibly" do so (Table 32). Even those who were not inclined to settle were obliged to think about the direction of their lives as Jews. "Decision necessarily turns on becoming more aware of personal preference and of the things for which one really wants one's life to stand." [8] Although most of the students did not reach a final decision, the constant pressures on them to choose among alternative courses of action helped clarify the nature of their Jewish identity.

In a Jewish Mirror

The students, however, not only emerged with a clearer understanding of where they stood as Jews. At the end of the year they were more proudly Jewish. But were they not proud Jews when they came? They were, in a qualified way. And it is precisely in regard to this qualification of their self-esteem that a basic change took place during the year's sojourn.

The American majority culture in which the students grew up attaches a certain stigma to the minority group of which they are members. [9] And inevitably in the process of socialization they absorb something of this derogatory view about their group, [10] even though it is modified through the prism of the American Jewish community with which they identify. They in effect see themselves in a distorted mirror held up by the non-Jewish majority.

In Israel the students found themselves for the first time in a society where Jews are in the majority and where they could look at themselves in a Jewish mirror. They emerged from this experience with heightened self-respect and pride in being Jewish and with less dependence on non-Jewish views about their Jewish identity.

If ever I had a Jewish inferiority complex, it was cured completely. I developed a greater pride in my people.

I was always proud to be a Jew—but it is as if only now I really understand why.

Before you came there's a feeling of not being sure of what you're proud of. Now I have a much more secure sense of pride.

After a year in a Jewish society the Jewishness of the students became less dependent on the Jew-Gentile contrast. In choosing courses of action open to American Jewry, the students attach less importance than before to activities directed to the non-Jewish community (Table 55). The course of action "improve relations between Jews and non-Jews," chosen by 42 per cent before arrival in Israel, was chosen by only 29 per cent toward the end of the sojourn. The course of action consistently chosen by the largest percentage of students was to "encourage the Jewish education of youth." Typical was the remark made by one of the students: "I am interested in educating the Jewish community and not in reforming Gentiles." A number of students expected to be more active than before in Jewish affairs on their return to the United States (Table 56).

Re-examination of American Identity

The sojourners' experience of life in Israel produced more changes in their Jewish than in their American subidentity. They developed, however, a greater awareness—as we have noted—of their Americanism. Moreover, their location outside the United States, the source of reference their new experiences provided, the self-scrutiny stimulated by the questioning of their hosts, all these brought about a re-evaluation and clarification of their American background. The process is reflected in the following remarks of a student:

I have become aware of my being an American in addition to becoming a Jew. I carefully follow the news in the American periodicals and in the Israeli press. I understand American policy more clearly and I am more likely to express my opinion. This has happened for a number of reasons. Israelis with whom I have had contact have regarded me either as an expert or a victim. In other words some were trying to convince me of the faults and drawbacks of American life. To answer both kinds of Israelis I needed information and well-developed arguments. I was also interested because for the first time in my life Americanism, not Judaism was the unusual element in my self. So, where I had studied and questioned Judaism in the past, I now studied and questioned Americanism.

The conclusions they reached in the process of a re-examination vary; some came to feel prouder than ever of their Americanism and others became more critical (Table 17). But whatever they might feel about it, the American elements in their identity—as some of them recognized for themselves—remain indelibly part of them. As one student put it at the end of the year's sojourn: "I know that I will always talk, act and think like an American."

Three Profiles of Change

The impact of the sojourn in Israel on the ethnic identity of the students can be concretely illustrated by depicting the changes which occurred in three students who were interviewed on various occasions during the year. They are here designated by the pseudonyms Joan Cohen, Esther Lewis, and John Abrahamson.[11] Joan and Esther represent the more common patterns of change, whereas John reflects the position of a small minority.

Joan Cohen. Joan Cohen grew up in a midwestern town with only about a dozen Jewish families. She had limited contact with Jews; her friends were in the main Gentiles who knew but little about Jews and their customs. "My friends in the United States would wish me Happy Easter and they didn't understand why I didn't celebrate Easter." She sometimes felt she would have liked to celebrate along with them.

Her Jewish education was meager in the extreme, and she reports that there is very little Jewish content in the lives of her parents. Her father shows acute insecurity with non-Jews in situations where he believes his Jewishness is likely to be a source of discrimination. "A hotel in my college town refused him a room once and he right away thought it was because his name was Cohen, but it wasn't so at all. They were full—that's all." Joan is aware of a similar oversensitivity on her own part. "I always felt a small chip on my shoulder that I guess I inherited from my father. I always had to get the best grades and to be the best behaved." In reply to a question as to what in her mind was the main factor in the development of antisemitism, where the alternatives provided were (1) the characteristics of the non-Jews, (2) the position of Jews as a minority among a non-Jewish majority, and (3) the characteristics of the Jews, she chooses the third alternative.

Although her relations with her non-Jewish friends were generally cordial, she felt that she was never "really an insider," that they looked upon her "as different" and that she did not "quite belong." There were a few Jewish students at her college and she eagerly sought their company. Among them was a girl who was better informed than most on Jewish matters, and Joan was ashamed of her own ignorance which became patent in discussions with this girl. When Joan expressed herself as eager to learn more about Judaism, the friend directed her attention to the One Year Program of Study at the Hebrew University.

En route to Israel, she writes (elaborating a reply in the questionnaire) in these terms of her aims and expectations for the sojourn:

I wish to live with other Jewish people and find out more about my own religion. . . . I will learn what Judaism can mean—I will learn Hebrew so that the religion will have more meaning . . . I know very little about my religion, yet respect its principles and want to know more. My family is not religious and we live just like our non-Jewish, American neighbors.

Of Israel and what it can mean for American Jewry she wrote: "A place where American Jews may go to 'find themselves' religiously, as it is hard to keep a 'Jewish' culture in America."

Among Jews, on the ship bound for Israel, she experienced for the first time a sense of release from the constant watchfulness imposed upon her by her Jewish identity in a non-Jewish world. In the first interview she described her reaction to the following incident:

Once I was making up my bed on the ship, and I was very aggravated with the steward because he didn't tuck in the sheets and I had to do it over myself. So I kept telling myself, "Don't be nasty to the steward, or he'll think all Jews are nasty." And then I realized where I was, that the steward was Jewish, we're all Jewish. . . . That steward can hate me for being me!

This sense of release was strengthened and deepened into a sense of belongingness after her arrival in Israel. She remarked in a later interview:

It's very nice to be able to go to synagogue and to go down the street and hear prayers. . . . It was so very strange walking—Erev Yom Kippur (Eve of the Day of Atonement)—to services on that evening. I was dressed up, of course, as I would have been in the States, but everyone else was too. It was so nice to see everyone else also going to services. Slightly awe-struck, I told the two girls I was with that it was "like being a Christian in the States on Christmas!"

What impressed Joan most of all about Israel was that here Jews pursued their lives in their own fashion unimpeded by a minority status. "I am not bothered here about the Jewish part of my personality or behavior."

Her observation of life in Israel altered the view she had held in the United States that Jewish identification could be expressed in religious terms only. "I'm more convinced that Judaism is more than a religion. I can understand a person who wants to identify without being religious." Speaking of an Israeli she had met on a tour of the country, she observed: "He disregards religion but feels for the Jewish homeland and is willing to die for it. Some time ago I would have said that the man wasn't Jewish because he wasn't religious."

The fact that most of her fellow-students in A.S.P. displayed some background knowledge on Jewish subjects made her keenly conscious again of her ignorance. She sought avidly to learn all she could. For a while—under the influence of friends in the group—she became religiously observant, but this observance declined later in the year.

The ambivalence she had known about her Jewishness in the United States largely disappeared. A question about what had been the most important change so far led her to make a self-assessment: "The recognition that I am a Jew —and all that means and implies—and the realization that I want to remain in the group. Eight months ago I was prepared to marry a Christian and ignore my heritage."

Whereas on board ship she had indicated that it was "unlikely" that she would ever settle in Israel, the reply toward the end of the sojourn moves up one rung on the ladder and is "may possibly." But the "possibility" is not strong— it is clear from what she says that Joan's orientation is toward life in the States.

Joan's intention now is to change her program of studies from a major in History to a major in Jewish Studies. Speaking of her plans for college and beyond, she says:

I think American Judaism needs help—if I'm any sample it needs help. I came here not knowing anything about Judaism and I think there shouldn't be a lot of people like me. . . . I'm going to go to Brandeis and I'm going to study Yahadut [Judaism] and I'm going to get a teaching certificate and I'm going to Minnesota to make sure there are less Jews like me that don't know they're Jewish. That's my mission.

At the end of the year Joan seemed headed for a life of stronger Jewish identification and more positive Jewish content. How far she will persist in this direction is likely to depend not a little on the social support she will receive in her American environment. While in Israel she was greatly influenced by a subgroup within A.S.P. which served her as a constant source of reference. Her attitudes need consolidation through anchorage in a group with Jewish purpose similar to that which influenced her in Israel.

The sojourn experience was a powerful stimulus to her Jewish development but could not by itself compensate for the lack of a Jewish education.

Esther Lewis. Unlike Joan Cohen, Esther Lewis enjoyed what she proudly describes as a "thorough traditional Jewish education." Her parents immigrated to America from Eastern Europe in their youth, met in New York where they married and set up their home. Esther was reared in the intensely Jewish atmosphere of an Orthodox home. Both parents were active Zionists and Esther recalls that from early childhood she was an interested listener to, and later a participant in, the frequent discussions around the family table on Israel. She excelled in both her Jewish and general studies at the Jewish day school she attended, and she found time in addition for activities in the Zionist religious youth organization in which she later occupied a position of leadership.

Members of the families of both parents had perished in the Holocaust in Europe. Esther recalls vividly the excitement in her home when they heard the announcement that Eichmann had been taken captive by Israelis, and she relates with what intense interest they subsequently followed the proceedings of the trial in Jerusalem.

There can be little doubt about the primacy of Jewish interests in her life. Explaining her position on the Jewish side of the Jewish-American scale, she notes: "I identify myself completely with the Jewish people. I also feel loyalty to the American government—as a citizen of the U.S. irrespective of my religion."

She is scornful of Jews "who try to assimilate" or who are "in constant dread of what the Gentiles may say about so-called Jewish behavior." Unlike Joan, who believes that the Jews may be at fault, Esther's view is that the main factor in the development of antisemitism is "the position of Jews as a minority among a non-Jewish majority."

She feels that there is some latent antisemitism in the United States, but passes lightly over antisemitic incidents she has encountered. Her view is that immigration to Israel should be motivated by what she regards as more positive reasons. "The overall feeling of being in America is a good feeling. I didn't feel I was persecuted or anything like that. . . . I think Jews should come to Israel for other reasons . . . Jews who want to live a Jewish life."

For Esther the visit to Israel was "a dream come true." Although there was much that was new and unexpected, she had read so much about Israel, had attended every Israeli exhibition and seen every film on Israel in New York, that at times she had the feeling "that I have visited these places before." She made a special point of visiting *Yad Va'shem* (the Holocaust memorial exhibition) soon after her arrival in Jerusalem.

Her knowledge of Hebrew placed her in the advanced class in the ulpan; she had no difficulty in conversing with the Israelis she met although it was apparent to her that they were at one and the same time impressed by her vocabulary and amused at her American intonation.

At the opening of the University term she threw herself with zest into several courses in the Hebrew University's Institute of Jewish Studies. Early in the term she had become friendly with an Israeli girl she had met at the Friday evening services conducted by students at the Hillel House. This friend frequently invited her to Friday evening meals at her home and also introduced her to a circle of religious students, members of the Yavneh organization. She describes as an "unforgettable experience" her visit along with some of these students to a religious kibbutz in the Beisan valley.

Although she agrees with her American fellow-students that the Israeli students "don't go out of their way to become acquainted with strangers" and "don't really understand us American Jews," her view of them is less critical, and she would temper the criticism of the others by drawing attention to what she regarded as the positive sides of the Israeli character. "The Israeli students are more serious and purposeful than Americans who are less concentrated and who are immature in comparison."

After the intense excitement of the first weeks had subsided, Esther continued to derive satisfaction from the fact that "I am now in a place where I feel as a Jew I really belong!" Although outspokenly critical of some aspects of Israeli life, her criticism reflects the sorrowful indignation of someone who feels herself deeply involved in all that related to the country. She observes that her Jewish education had provided her with a perspective allowing for a more understanding assessment of Israel. "I felt more of a warmness and closeness, was less of an outsider. With the background I had in Jewish history I understood what was going on in the country more (than the other students) when I arrived."

She was distressed to find that an uncle and aunt in Israel contemplate immigration to America. She ponders the irony of the situation. While she is seeking ways of settling in Israel, her relatives are intent on leaving. "They don't know the difference between living in a Jewish state and living in a place where you're a minority." But how is it that they do not know, she asks herself. "My uncle and aunt come from Europe and they must just have forgotten.

Maybe people forget. So it could be my uncle forgot and takes things for granted here which when he comes to America he will suddenly miss."

Describing Israel as "the heart of Judaism," she feels that the year in Israel has shown her the difference between living at the heart, the center, and living on the periphery. The consonance between general and Jewish activities is particularly to her liking. "Here it is such a synthesis of everyday life and Jewish life together. It makes a big difference."

The sojourn in Israel had added a further dimension to her Jewishness. The intensity of feeling which accompanies this Jewishness found expression in the interview before her departure from Israel.

I was proud before. Perhaps before I might have seen Judaism more as a religion. Now I don't see it less as a religion but also as a nation. . . . the national part of it, that I didn't see before I mean, I saw it, of course, but I didn't feel it as strongly. I feel different. . . . I understand and see different parts of Judaism that I didn't feel before. And they're mainly positive . . . so it sort of makes me feel better. I knew academically that it was also a nation. Now that I feel it . . . it gives me a sense of belonging. I feel part of a specific nation in the world.

Toward the end of the sojourn she expresses an intention to settle: "Israel is the homeland of the Jewish people. Feeling myself a Jew it appears to follow logically that I live in Israel if it is at all possible." She admits at the same time that her roots in the States are deep and the family ties close. She would like to transplant her family but doubts whether she can convey to anyone who has not passed through the experience of the year in Israel a proper appreciation of what Israel means in Jewish life.

(On her return to New York, Esther married an Orthodox student with views about Israel similar to her own. In a letter written in 1968 she reported that they were planning to settle in Israel.)

John Abrahamson. John Abrahamson is a third generation American. He says that his parents readily identify with the Jewish community but that there is nothing particularly Jewish about their home. As he describes it, their Jewishness expresses itself merely in the fact that in their social life they consort mainly with Jews, that they attend services at the Temple on the New Year and Day of Atonement, and that they contribute to Jewish charitable causes. Of his own Jewish education he has this to tell: "My formal religious education consisted of five years of Sunday School in a Reform Temple. . . . I felt more of a bond with Judaism as a result of my name and facial structure than I did in response to what I learned."

He adds that his understanding of Judaism had altered somewhat as a result of a course he had taking the previous year in comparative religion. "I began to see the beauty and spirit of Judaism, even defended it in the face of anti-Semitic comments made by non-Jewish friends; could feel a slight sense of belongingness." He regards Jews as a religious group only.

During the course of a trip around the world his parents visited Israel. While in Jerusalem they contacted the son of friends who was a student in the American Student Program. He spoke so enthusiastically about his experiences in Israel that John's parents there and then decided that their son should come to the Hebrew University the following year. John was not averse to a year abroad although his own preference would have been for France rather than Israel. "My thoughts about Israel involved distasteful associations with people as well as ideas. The idea of 'longing for the homeland' or the necessity for an escape from unkind society was not in my background, or was cynically regarded."

John arrived in Israel later than the other members in the American Student Program and joined them at the ulpan at which they were studying Hebrew. The lack of previous acquaintanceship with the A.S.P. group, which by now had attained a measure of cohesiveness, accentuated the feeling of being a lonely outsider in the unfamiliar environment in which he now found himself. "Ignorance of the language, completely new people and surroundings, initial exclusion from the already acquainted A.S.P. group in the ulpan rendered me unhappy and lonesome." In this disconsolate mood he could share few of the enthusiasms of his fellow-students, and at the same time he looked with a more jaundiced eye than did most of them on what they too regarded as irritating phenomena—"the bureaucratic inefficiency, the crowds pushing at bus stops."

His spirits lifted somewhat on his first excursion into the country. He had in the meantime become friendly with several of his American fellow-students and the joint excursion solidified this friendship. What he now saw of the country impressed him, and he found himself infected with some of the excitement of his companions even if the places they visited did not evoke the same associations for him as they did for members of the group who knew more about the historical background of Israel then he. Later, together with a friend, he spent a weekend at a kibbutz in the Valley of Jezreel, and returned with high praise for the "sense of idealistic purpose" as well as the warm hospitality of the settlers. But, although not religiously observant himself, he was disconcerted at the absence of a religious character to the Sabbath at the kibbutz, and at the indifference of the settlers to matters of religion. He was puzzled as to how he should categorize the Jewishness of the Israelis he was now meeting. "I have always thought of Judaism as a religion." He discussed the question with other American students when he returned to Jerusalem, but could not accept what he termed their "national approach" to the issue. He found himself irritated by their constant reference to "the future of the Jewish people," and he adds: "What is more important is the future of *Judaism*." This he said with some heat in the interview, but then paused and observed somewhat apologetically: "If my opinions sound terribly inconsistent and confuséd, please forgive me. The problem is that I *am* very confused and bewildered with respect to the entire issue."

A visit at about this time to *Yad Va'shem* deepened this reflective mood. He had not imagined that he would be stirred as intensely as he was, and as he left the hall he found himself in silent agreement with the student at his side who remarked to him that the meaning of the Israel of today could only be fully comprehended if viewed in the perspective of the Holocaust. "Surprisingly I had never consciously connected the holocaust to the birth of Israel in more than a superficial chronological manner."

After the months at the ulpan, spent mainly in the company of American students, he awaited the opening of the university's academic year in November with eager anticipation. He was particularly interested in getting to know the Israeli students; apart from his visit to the kibbutz the contact with Israelis was limited to a few superficial encounters. At all times a serious student, he became absorbed in some of the courses he attended even though he followed the lectures with difficulty because of his limited Hebrew (He was surprised at the progress he had made in the months at the ulpan, since he knew only a few words when he arrived in Israel). But he was critical of the lack of a campus life such as he had known in the United States and sorely disappointed at what seemed to him an insuperable difficulty in establishing friendships with the Israeli students.

My contacts with Israelis were very limited. (My roommate was a new immigrant from Rumania so doesn't count). I was in a couple of classes with real Israelis. . . . I found that my attempt to form close relationships were not succeeding and that even casual relationship with Israelis were difficult to form in comparison with Americans. . . . I gave up attempts to find Israeli friends and spent more time with Americans. The more I did this the more I felt my Americanism return.

In this period of frustration in the area of social contact he became highly critical of the Israeli students.

While the university is a fine academic institution, it seems to have students more concerned with job training than intellectual discovery or application of knowledge to solve the nation's social problems (some of which Israelis seemed not to want to recognize as such).

During one of the university vacations John traveled together with another American student to Turkey and Greece. The contrast provided by a non-Jewish environment made him aware of psychological advantages in a Jewish society which he had tended to overlook.

The impact of moving from the Jewish society of Israel was startling. I felt a sort of apologetic fear which I remembered from times previous to visiting Israel. When my friend displayed any actions which resembled the pushy stereotype of the Jew, or loudly announced our place of temporary residence, I balked. . . . It was with a sense of relief that I re-entered Israel—I felt secure, welcome.

His experience in Turkey and Greece also made him look somewhat more benignly at Israeli "bureaucracy and inefficiency" which he had hitherto compared with American standards only.

In the remaining months John's views about Israel mellowed further. He states that "Israel has a very important place in Jewish life," but adds, "unlike my Israeli counterparts I do not think that 'this is the only place for you.'" He has no intention of ever settling in Israel and feels exasperated at the questions addressed to him on the subject by Israelis after even the most casual acquaintanceship. "Everywhere I went the question was 'How long have you been in Israel?' followed by 'Are you planning to stay?' If Israelis realized what a negative influence this line of questions is, I am sure that they would desist."

Although he admits that there are exceptions among them and recalls in particular his experience at the kibbutz, Israelis continue to be the subject of critical comment and he feels remote from them.

I feel more "at home" with Americans than Israelis. I often find them petty, crude, insolent and concerned with things that do not concern me. The common bond of the appelation "Jew" does not seem sufficient to overcome the schism created by the lack of common experiences.

Indeed, as the time for return draws nearer he increasingly stresses his Americanism: "I prefer American music, friends, movies and food. If anything the year in Israel has strengthened my feeling for America."

When John was reinterviewed in the States, he said he

had been surprised at the way the Six Day War had moved him to "examine my feelings as a Jew." He looked back upon the sojourn as a positive experience which, he stated, helped him in this re-examination. He asserts that whereas he once had regarded his being Jewish as having no necessary relation to Israel, he no longer holds this view. "When we are confronted with a situation which threatens the existence of Israel, no Jew can stand aside." He still believes, however, that Judaism, as he interprets it, has a better future in the United States:

I found that I could see few elements of religion in Israel that I could identify with in a positive way. I feel that the main problem of the Jewish religion in the States is to keep pace with the times, something which it is doing much better than the Jewish religion of Israel.

Summing up, he says: "I found the country itself highly inspirational, yet the people populating it highly uninspirational. The lack of courtesy extended to me as an American rubbed me the wrong way."

There is, however, no rancor now in his feeling about Israelis, "I guess the time since my return has tended to remove some of the bitterness and sharpness from this opinion. From a distance you can objectively see the tremendous progress which has been made, without being a part of the confusion of an ongoing process." He says that as a result of his sojourn his interest in Israel's welfare "has grown tremendously." He expects to visit Israel again but certainly not to settle there, declaring "I hold unerasable identification as an American which is cemented in ties to family and friends."

CHAPTER 11

The Students and the Six Day War: In Face of a Common Danger

The students in the 1966–1967 American Student Program were nearing the end of their sojourn when the Middle East crisis assumed serious proportions in May 1967. Egyptian troops marched into Sinai and massed on Israel's southern border, the Straits of Tiran were closed to Israeli shipping, and leaders in the Arab countries grew bolder in their threats to destroy Israel.

As war seemed imminent, cables reached the students from their parents urging them to return immediately; furthermore the United States Embassy advised American citizens to leave. A meeting of students was called, and although no formal resolution was taken, the consensus of the group was clear. The minority of waverers fell into line with the norm which was thus established in the stranger group. Moreover, the support of fellow-students facing the same predicament enabled them to withstand the pressure from parents. Not a single student left.

The Six Day War, along with the crisis which preceded it and its aftermath, stirred even the most marginal Jews in distant communities—more so than any event since the establishment of the State of Israel. It affected all the more profoundly the students who were on the spot witnessing —alongside the local population—the hour to hour progression of developments, including the shelling of the city in which they lived. The factors in the situation which so deeply influenced the students merit some attention.

The students had been infants when Israel came into being. Unlike their parents they did not remember a world without a Jewish state, and they took its existence for granted. The threat to Israel's very existence suddenly illumined, as if with lightning flash, the depth of its significance to them as Jews.

When there was a chance that Israel would be destroyed I suddenly became aware of how vital Israel is to the Jewish people.

My existence as a Jew was being threatened simultaneously with the threat against Israel.

I'd say the biggest impact of the Six Day War on me was the realization (the knowledge was there before June 1967) that the destruction of Israel meant the end of our one sign of hope in modern Jewish existence. American Jews couldn't live without Israel.

In addition, the unstinting and unhesitating support extended to Israel by Jews everywhere underlined still further for the students—as it did for Israelis—the sense of interdependence and of mutual responsibility. "I feel that in essence we are one people striving to exist together."

The crisis reactivated the memory of the Holocaust. Although the students belonged to a generation born after the Holocaust, the memory of this tragedy was embedded in their consciousness, and the Arab threats aroused ominous associations. Eighty-seven per cent indicated that they had been reminded during these weeks of the Holocaust (Table 57).

We feared similar destruction could happen.

Whenever Jews are threatened the holocaust comes into your thoughts.

Feeling of we can't and won't let it happen again.

At the same time they observed the contrast between the position of a beleaguered but self-reliant state and a powerless European Jewry.

I thought of the totally different response of the Israelis to a threat to their very existence. Of course, the Israelis had many more advantages.

I also thought that the only way the holocaust could *possibly* have been prevented would have been if there was a strong sovereign Jewish state.

Their identification with the Israelis was intense and complete; they saw them as Jewish warriors defending their people from a position of strength without need to depend on others.

It would be nice if people would live together—but Jews have been used and misused too much in history and especially in this century. *We* have to be strong and depend on *ourselves— we've* been the world's scapegoat for too long. The Six Day War has caused me to believe this strongly. The holocaust should have and did show me this but the Six Day War and its preceding and post-war days gave me an example I could see before my own eyes. (Italics added.)

The students shared the elation of the Israelis with the victory and their ecstacy knew no bounds when they now found themselves able to pray at the Western Wall. They saw the Six Day War within a historical time perspective as a "Jewish war" rather than just an "Israeli war." In particular, that part of the struggle which concerned Jerusalem and the Western Wall emphasized for them, as for Israelis, the Jewish dimension of the war.

With the announcement of the capture of Jerusalem I again became a Jew. . . . The picture of the young soldier praying at the Wailing Wall became the symbol of the country; *we* were a nation of Jews fighting for *our* own existence and for the existence of Jews everywhere. (Italics added.)

Alongside Israelis in Danger

The decision not to leave the country, to remain in Israel alongside the Israelis, had farreaching psychological implications.[1] So a student, who had been weighing for some time the pros and cons of settlement, described how he was suddenly confronted with an unexpected test of his relationship to Israel.

The Six Day War was a frightening, moving, and compelling experience. The "test" of commitment as such came not with the onset of the war but rather with the two or three weeks preceding it, when there were clear warnings and advisements to get out. I chose not to, mainly because I felt that if I were in Israel for any reason other than to see "another" country, I could only demonstrate a commitment by staying (given, of course, that the Israelis did not demand that we leave). So the war took on the most real of implications for me and compelled me to regard Israel and its fate in a yet more intimate light. It strengthened my resolve to make my relation to Israel a more permanent and binding one.

And other students wrote in the same vein:

The crisis has also pushed the dilemma of my identification to a crisis. I chose to stay in Israel during the War—and now I know I will always choose Israel as my first home.

I felt that I could not leave no matter what threatened. It was a moral question for me; if I abandoned the country now, how could I ever return with a clear conscience to live here. If I wanted to settle in Israel, I would have to face the war along with every other Israeli.

Having faced the Israel vs. home country confrontation under such circumstances and resolving it in such a manner . . . was actually far more important than it appeared to be, especially in respect to future aliyah.

The students volunteered for a variety of civilian defense preparations. They helped fortify air-raid shelters, they prepared bandages at the Hadassah hospital, they sorted and distributed mail in the absence of the postal employees, and they assisted in the harvest in the kibbutzim.

Strangers no Longer

The confrontation along with Israelis of a common danger and the participation in defense activities brought a sense of deeper involvement in Israel and its destiny. The Israelis too—impressed by the response of Jews everywhere —looked upon them in a new light, as fellow-Jews upon whom they could depend in every contingency. During the days of crisis and of war the barriers between the students and Israelis were suddenly lowered; the students ceased to feel themselves strangers in Israel. In the questionnaire responses they give frequent and delighted expression to the sense of being "at home" and belonging.

My feeling of unity has greatly increased because I chose to stay and I did volunteer work in Jerusalem and on a kibbutz. So I feel and felt part of the people's war effort.

I feel that this country is my home. I feel that I belong.

I felt a lot more comfortable here, a feeling that I can belong and become part of the country.

I feel a close attachment to the Israelis as it was "our" war.

I've always loved the country, but I felt I really couldn't belong here permanently—that I would possibly not be needed. I don't feel that way now.

The students were asked whether, in comparison with their feelings prior to the war, they now felt more, less, or as Jewish, Israeli, or American as before. The responses showed a substantial change in the direction of feeling more Israeli and more Jewish (Table 58).

Pride and Respect

The students not only witnessed the valor of Israel's soldiers; they were also impressed by the unfaltering morale of the civilian population during the crisis. They saw Israelis at their best; their admiration grew and their criticism decreased. The words "pride in" and "respect for" appear repeatedly.

Made me realize that under pressure they function marvellously and has increased my respect for them manifold.

I saw that in a crisis people were wonderful. They helped one another, cooperated, did what they could. The army was amazingly organized and made me proud just like everyone else.

Felt before idealism was dead and Israelis apathetic about everything. I made a mistake.

Even students who regarded themselves as antimilitaristic were impressed. "The reactions of the soldiers I have met is quite antimilitary. They fought hard but are quite affected by and sensitive about what happened."

A certain ambivalence, however, remained in the attitude of some of the students towards Israelis. In some areas they were still critical of Israelis. "I am still bitter about certain traits and stupidities. I am proud of their bravery and determination and army efficiency. Shame it doesn't spread to other areas."

Some students also questioned whether the closer relationship with Israelis would last after the tension eased. "During the crisis I felt closer to them, and they, I think, to me. I'm not sure that this feeling is continuing so strongly after the easing off of tension."

Impetus to Settle

The decision made during the crisis not to leave Israel coupled with the subsequent impact of the War helped to clarify the students' feelings about eventual settlement. The decision to settle in Israel is, as we have noted earlier, rarely a sudden, overnight resolution; it is the culmination of a gradual, stepwise process. The sojourn generally results at most in an *intention* to settle. The events of June, however, took the majority of students one or two steps forward from where they had previously stood, resulting in a greater readiness for aliyah on the part of students in 1967 than by their fellows who were in the 1965–1966 group. Thus, twenty-eight of the thirty-three who completed a questionnaire after the Six Day War indicated that what they had experienced during this period had either reinforced a previous intention (without necessarily resulting, as yet, in a final decision) or had at least strengthened the possibility of settlement (even if no firm intention was reached).

A new psychological climate surrounded the whole question of immigration. In the wake of the war the call for large-scale immigration from the free countries assumed additional urgency. The students too became more convinced of this need and wholeheartedly subscribed to the prevailing view. They no longer expressed irritation at the questioning of the Israelis on the subject. Instead some experienced a sense of guilt that they could not immediately respond.

Whereas in the past I thought aliyah was right for me and I wouldn't encourage it for others (necessarily), I have since turned missionary, especially among American Jews. I find it harder to leave Israel at a time I feel so close to it and at a time when every Jew here counts. I plan to return sooner than I expected.

CHAPTER 12

On Returning to the United States: Looking Inward and Outward

As soon as they set foot again on American shores, the students cease to be representatives of their country, guests singled out as "American" by their hosts. The salience of their Americanism declines (Table 59). At the same time several of the students indicate how much more "at home" they feel again as Americans in the United States as contrasted with the "strangeness" they experienced in Israel.

On the other hand, they are once again placed in juxtaposition as Jews with a non-Jewish majority. The contrast of the first year back in the United States with the year in a Jewish society enhances their Jewish awareness (Table 60). Thus, a student remarks:

Being in Israel lessens one's feelings of being Jewish as apart from being something else. In the U.S. this distinction is heightened.

They report a further clarification of the role of Jewishness in their lives.

I am even more aware of the fact that my Jewishness is my primary self-awareness.

I am more willing to acknowledge my Jewishness. I accept it in myself.

The students are unanimous in feeling that the stimulating experience of a year in a different culture has given them a broader outlook. When they compare themselves with their peers who did not have the benefit of a year overseas, they realize how much they have changed.

I think this is what happened to all of us—you come home after the year eager to see the family, your friends. At your first meeting with the friends everything is fine but you soon realize how much you changed your thoughts. They were in America all their life, and their thought—like all other Americans.

Reappraisal of Life in America

While the students were still in Israel they had begun to review life in the United States within the new framework of comparison provided by their sojourn. But now, when their day-by-day life is again in this American milieu, a more intense significance attaches to the reappraisal. Some look at American life and character more appreciatively, others more critically, but it is no longer taken for granted as the only way of the world: "I realize now that I led a sheltered life living in the States. Before my trip I was really quite unaware of important differences between the United States and another country."

Events in the United States introduce a more somber note into the responses of students questioned in December 1968 as compared with the responses to the questionnaire in May–June 1967. They had been deeply disturbed by the assassinations of Martin Luther King and Robert Kennedy, by the dimming of the hopes these two men represented in their eyes, by gnawing doubts about the war in Vietnam, by the increase of violent crime in the cities, by the manifestations of virulent antisemitism in the ranks of Black

Power protagonists. There is a sense of disillusionment in 1968 which was absent in 1967 and in the years which preceded it. What the students now find stands out in marked contrast to what they remember of their experience in Israel. A disconsolate student writes cryptically: "Felt lost on my return, bewildered, air so dirty, life (N.Y.C.) so crowded. Noticed more the muggings etc." And another states: "If anything, the forces alienating me from American society seem on the upsurge; and I long for what I remember in Israeli society of the esprit de corps and value of something beyond crass materialism."

They also tend to reexamine the Jewish position in the light of the changed conditions. Thus a student, after declaring that "fear and violence in U.S. cities are worse or seem worse after being in Israel," proceeds to review the "rebuffs" administered to Jews in the Civil Rights movement and comes to the conclusion that "it seems a law of history that the Jews work for others and get kicked in the teeth; it's about time we work for ourselves."

A number of students gave expression to a sympathetic understanding of the desire of Blacks for the assertion of their identity and their striving for the equality of their group. At the same time this served to underline for some of them the legitimacy of their own concern with their Jewish identity. The students take a more serious view of antisemitism in the United States in 1968 than in the preceding years, but few reach so extreme a conclusion as does the student who remarks: "I see a most frightening prospect of anti-semitism led by both Negroes and WASPS. I honestly don't see very much of a future for American Jews. I fear the American Jew's inability or fear of seeing and preparing himself for every eventuality, because 'it can happen here.'"

Views on American Jewish Life

A number of the students were critical of American Jewry and American Jewish life before they went to Israel. They are more so after their return. They are more selective about the Jewish activities in which they choose to participate and do not easily reconcile themselves to the forms of Jewish existence in the United States after having tasted of what they term the more "natural" Jewish life in Israel. The expressions of Jewish life in America seem to them to be primarily religious and do not cover the broad spectrum they found characteristic of Jewishness in Israel. Their view of the American Jewish community is pessimistic; it is seen as moving increasingly in the direction of assimilation, its future is "dismal," and they maintain (with some dissentient voices) that Judaism can have "no meaningful future outside of Israel." Several state that they would like their yet unborn children to grow up in the "healthier Jewish atmosphere" of Israel.

There are, of course, gradations and individual differences in the attitude to American Jewish life. At one end of the continuum are students who are unreservedly pessimistic in their outlook about the future of the community.

Since my stay in Israel, I tend to see the American Jewish community as a "fossilized remnant," a dead "bunch" as compared with the Israeli community. I feel that efforts to rejuvenate it are wasted.

It has no meaningful future outside of Israel. I feel that a very small proportion of Jews will survive the experience of the modern world as Jews in the traditional sense, if in any sense at all, except in Israel.

The future of American Jewry is dismal. The young and dedicated will settle in Israel and the vast majority will assimilate in the American culture.

Except for the orthodox and zionistic, American Jewry is on its way out. A sorry prediction, but that's how I feel.

I guess it's only since my return from Israel that *I feel* that I'm in the *galut* [Exile]. I've lived all my life in the U.S. but it's only since I've been in Israel that I feel what it is to be in the *galut.*

Some students limit the criticism more specifically to what American Jewish life lacks for them. Thus, a student, a devoutly religious Zionist keenly interested in what she terms "creative Jewish living," reflects that, although American Judaism may not meet her demands, it may do so for other Jews.

I have found that my dissatisfaction with Jewish life in America has been sharpened by living in Israel. But I recognize that the problems it poses for me are not shared by most American Jews and that the institutionalized American Judaism which I cannot accept does fulfill the needs of most of its members.

And others similarly point to what they see as deficiencies affecting their own way of living—or that of their children. Several express this concern about the continued Jewishness of the next generation.

Although I am sure that I am capable of continuing my religious observance in America, I am wary of trying to bring up children there. I am not sure that I could provide them with the feeling toward Judaism which I have.

American Judaism is essentially religious, and has little room for Jewish national and cultural expression. Therefore it has little room for us.

Still others seek ways for expressing in the United States the broader conception of being Jewish that they have acquired. "My interests as a Jew are inevitably expanded and create a certain amount of need to express myself in these terms in the local Jewish environment."

Although the students repeatedly declare Israel to be "the center of Jewish life" and recognize the interdependence and mutual responsibility that exists between it and American Jewry (as well as other Diaspora Jewries), what is conspicuously absent from the view of Jewish life most of them hold is a conception of an integrated Jewish world in which the various communities are interlocking parts. They tend to think in terms of two (or more) Jewish worlds. For some, the world of Israel holds the hope of a Jewish future whereas the American Jewish world is doomed to gradual dissolution; for others, the American Jewish community contains within itself the potential for a creative survival, and a vague notion exists of the "inspiration" the Jewish center in Israel will provide. But essentially they remain two separate worlds in the minds of the students and there is no clear view of the interpenetration of mutual influences. The dilemma into which this approach thrusts some of the students is reflected in the following remarks:

My view of American Jewry is still a troubled one, perhaps more so since my return from Israel. I am torn between commitment to a thriving American Jewish life that would in a sense "prove" that Jews can live here and preserve Judaism as well in a situation unparalleled in the history of the world, and commitment to an ideal Ben-Gurionized world in which every Jew would ultimately see that his future lies in Israel and that no other land is ever totally "safe" for Jews, whether because of overt persecution or the more subtle type of sincere absorption and acculturation which in the end would be fatal toward Judaism though kind to Jews.

A state of confusion exists in my view of the place of Israel in Jewish life. . . . While I definitely cannot acknowledge the validity of a Jewish life *devoid* of Israel (à la American Council for Judaism), I am still uncertain as to the nature of what such a place should be.

A similar dichotomy characterizes the thinking of the students on the subject of the aliyah of American Jews. Such aliyah is seen as benefiting the individuals concerned who find self-fulfillment in Israel or as contributing to the consolidation of Israel. It is never seen as part of a process that may set into motion forces calculated to vitalize American Jewish life.

Among the changes remarked on by some of the students are those in their relationship with non-Jews. They are less defensive and less inclined to be apologetic on any Jewish issue. It would seem that the fuller cognizance of the equality of their Jewish group among peoples (as exemplified by the status of Israel) has induced in them a sense of equality as members of that group in the encounter with non-Jews. "I feel that I have no need to introduce apologetics into discussions of Israel, Judaism, or related subjects either with fellow-Jews or non-Jews. On such matters I let my opinion be expressed, like or not, and accepted or rejected on face value."

Only a few are sufficiently conscious of the subtle change that has taken place within themselves in the social encounter with non-Jews to remark on it spontaneously, but another area of Jew-Gentile relationships is the subject of heated comment. During the crisis of May 1967 preceding the Six Day War, there had been bitter criticism in American Jewish circles of the failure of some of the Christian organizations to rally to Israel's side when its destruction was threatened, and, in the period that followed, rebukes by the Security Council of the United Nations directed against Israel (without condemnation of the actions of the terrorist gangs who provoked the retaliation) intensified the feeling that Israel was standing alone. The students questioned in 1968 give widespread expression to a feeling that Jews must fend for themselves and cannot rely upon the Gentile world.

The Six-Day War convinced me once and for all that only self-reliance has any relevance in our day and age. The War showed me that the Jew has remained just as alienated from the Gentile nations as he always was, but this time he can fend for himself—or die in the attempt.

I believe more strongly that we have to depend on ourselves. It's a little shocking but I really think that the world would have let Israel be exterminated. It's good to have friendly relations with countries but you can only depend on yourself in the end.

I have become acutely aware of not being dependent on any well-wishers or comforters to come to the support of the Jewish people (or perhaps any particular group) during a crisis. I guess it seems natural that no one is going to risk his own neck for others, no matter how much thoughts, feelings, or words are to the contrary.

I am bothered by the non-Jewish world, which is sympathetic with Israel if it appears that Israel is about to be destroyed, but is appalled by an Israeli victory.

The Irritations Forgotten

With the passage of time their attitude toward Israel, favorable on departure, becomes even more highly favorable. The attitude toward Israelis also improves, although the feeling for the country still maintains the higher degree of favorableness (Tables 61 and 62).

For some students the events of the period doubtlessly contributed to the more favorable picture of Israelis. But other factors were also at work. At a distance the irritations experienced in the daily contact with Israelis are no longer salient. Although the students still have reservations about the social graces of their former hosts, this aspect no longer looms large in the general picture they retain of the sojourn. The following statements are typical of the responses to the question whether the year back in the States has brought about any change in their views of Israel and Israelis.

I forget the small things about them that bothered me, and only recall their good, general qualities.

The bad things fade about the country and the people and the better things stand out more.

I seem to remember the good aspects of life there and to have forgotten the disadvantages or problems.

When in Israel I was often critical of lack of efficiency, backward conditions, etc. In the U.S. I am more likely to think of the Israelis' great achievements.

When asked to what they thought back with most longing, ten of the students mention Jerusalem. Typical of the enthusiastic statements: "I miss Israel greatly—more than I ever imagined I would. I love Jerusalem and all that it encompasses." "I love Jerusalem. I'm simply spellbound by it. If I settle in Israel, it will be there." Apart from being the city in which they had lived during the year of their sojourn, it represented for a number of them the quintessence of that Jewishness rooted in the Jewish past which they sought in Israel. Several of the religious students refer nostalgically to the "Shabat in Jerusalem."

Their sense of identification with Israel remains strong; they are as sensitive as they were to an insult of Israel, seeing it as an insult against themselves. Outside of Israel there is a slight tendency to accept praise of Israel more readily than before as praise for themselves (Tables 63 and 64).

When the students resume their studies in the United States, the universities they enter provide a new basis of comparison by which the Hebrew University is re-evaluated. While they were in Israel the students had admired the level of Jewish studies, but their satisfaction with the instruction in other departments had varied. Even when the academic rating they now accord the Hebrew University is high, there is still some criticism, albeit moderated in tone, of the absence of a campus life, the difficulty in establishing social relations with Israeli students, and the administrative arrangements.

My attitude towards Hebrew University has improved. When I attended the University I had spent two years at a small college. I felt the impersonality and lack of organization was something limited to Hebrew University but now that I am at a large University for graduate school I realize that the problems are prevalent at most large universities.

There I found certain specific courses and teachers to be excellent, yet I was dissatisfied with and critical of the courseload and the impersonality of a large university. (This latter, of course, is not exclusively a problem of the Hebrew University.)

As for the Hebrew University, my overall view is favorable, especially as I become more aware of its actual stature (considerably large) in the academic world. However, time cannot erase the recollections of how frustrating the campus situation was at the student-level.

I have come more and more to appreciate some of the uniqueness of the courses I was taking there. I have come across enough administrative bungling in the last two years to convince me the Hebrew University has no monopoly though it has more than its share.

Some students who had considered staying beyond the year in order to embark upon a regular course of studies for a degree at the Hebrew University refer ruefully to the cumbersome requirements which daunted all but the most determined among them.

The Hebrew University, I continue to feel, is out of touch with foreign students who want to spend an extended period of study there. They make it unduly difficult and tedious to obtain a B.A. and/or transfer credits. This is quite unfortunate since "davka" (despite it all) those students most interested in aliyah are discouraged from continuing on another year of study in Israel.

In retrospect, as during the sojourn, their studies at the Hebrew University are not in the center of the total experience. A student who was once highly critical of the courses he audited now refers to the University in more temperate tones, and adds: "I was more critical of the University while I was in attendance there. Now it doesn't play a very large role in my total view of my sojourn." When students think back about the Hebrew University their sentiment for it derives—as when first they came to it—not so much from its quality as a teaching institution as from the fact that it is located in Jerusalem.

What some of the students moreover feel is that for them the merit of the Hebrew University lay precisely in its differentness from their American university, that it provided, as a student put it, "an education quite divergent from the typical American college," and that as a result they obtained a more variegated learning experience than their peers who did not venture beyond the confines of their own country.

The Decision to Settle—"Driving" and "Restraining" Forces

Looking back upon Israel from the vantage point of the United States, a few of the students have become more intent on settlement in Israel (Table 65).

The slow, step-by-step progression toward an intention to settle is again reflected in the changes recorded at the end of the year in the States. Of the twenty-nine students in the 1965 A.S.P. replying to this question, fifteen report no change after their departure from Israel; among the fourteen who have changed, ten have moved upward on the five-rung ladder, eight of the ten ascending one rung only (Table 66).

What were the forces bringing some of the students nearer to an intention to settle? Back in the United States the organization of the impressions gained during the sojourn took place—usually around the more favorable items. The attractiveness of Israel was thus enhanced, and the "driving forces" toward settlement were consequently strengthened. At the same time an even greater contribution to the progression toward an intention to settle seems to have been produced—as an analysis of the statements of the students shows—by a weakening of the "restraining forces," i.e., the factors previously militating against settlement.

During the sojourn, they were concerned about the attitude of their parents—often likely to be one of opposition —to a decision to settle in Israel. Even if there was no opposition, the thought of parting bore heavily on the students. On their return to the United States they realized that the year of separation had given them a measure of independence from their parents. The thought of parting no longer appeared so formidable.

The new framework of comparison within which they now view the United States results at times in a more critical view and in a lesser reluctance to leave the country. The comforts of American life are also differently evaluated, and whereas some rejoice to return to them, others find themselves more ready than they had thought to forego them.

I was always afraid to commit myself because I felt I'd never be able to tear myself away from the place where I was brought up. Now I see I can do it very easily.

I want to complete my doctoral studies before returning to Israel. Settling in Israel doesn't seem any longer as a great sacrifice of my comforts and American privileges. I intend to give it a serious try soon.

The atmosphere of disillusionment in the United States of 1968 has reduced the reluctance even further. "I have experienced disillusion and depression concerning the situation of the United States. Idealistic, unafraid, forward-looking Israel is very attractive to me."

Whether they actually take a decision depends in no small measure on the support and example of friends around them. "Today I talked to B, and he too has decided to come on aliya. It sure is reassuring to know that some others feel the same as I do. Also it means that I won't be so alone when I do come to Israel." If they have the necessary social reinforcement—and in particular if friends decide to settle—the chances that the decision will be maintained are much greater. The decision is reached at the end of a process of development in a group context and requires group support to survive. Furthermore, the difficulties the students had encountered in establishing social contact with Israelis underscored for them the need to come to Israel with a congenial social group of their own.

Other students, on the return to the United States, move further away from the intention to settle. In Israel the prevailing norm of the stranger group, more particularly so at the Institute, was to declare that the possibility of personal settlement was not excluded, that, at least, it was under favorable consideration. The retraction of the intention to settle was admitted by these students only after the return to the United States when they were removed from the social pressures to which they had been subject in Israel.

Plans to immigrate can generally be implemented only after some years. Continued residence in the United States allows for the operation of contrary influences and also may result in commitments (such as marriage or profession) militating against settlement in Israel.

I feel an obligation to help Israel—to ensure her existence as a homeland for all Jews. But I remain undecided because I have a family here, and more important, because I plan to marry someone who has not been exposed to Israel the way I have and therefore will require some convincing before we can move there.

Only if the decision is constantly buttressed within a group framework is it likely to withstand the corroding influences of time and place.

Reactions of Students in the United States to Six Day War

The reactions of the students of the 1965–1966 American Student Program who followed the events of May and June 1967 from a distance lack the intensity of the 1966–1967 group who were on the spot. They too, however, reflect a sense of strong identification and a readiness to be of help. Several of the students indicated that they were volunteering for service in Israel (and subsequently carried out their intentions).

While Israel is at war I feel it incumbent upon me to come to her aid as a volunteer as do many others who have spent some time in Israel. It is questionable whether so many American youths would feel so strongly had they not had the experience of being in Israel.

The present crisis has shown me how deep my feeling and attachment is for Israel. I hope to be there this summer to help in whatever way I can.

This was midyear 1967. In the period that followed there was a growing recognition in ever wider Jewish circles of the importance of Western aliyah for Israel. The students questioned in December 1968 are very emphatic in stressing the need for such aliyah but tend to be skeptical about whether any appreciable number of American Jews would immigrate. Thus, a student, who is planning to settle, remarks:

I do believe that aliyah from the West is desirable. However, I am not overly optimistic about the possibility of a significant number of American Jews emigrating to Israel. I feel from my acquaintances and contacts that most American Jews are not even potential aliyah material. My year in Israel impressed me with the importance of aliyah, as well as all the problems it entails, both for the immigrants and the state.

CHAPTER 13

The Student as Immigrant

Of the students who attended the Leadership Institute
during the twenty-one years of its existence, it is estimated
that over 1,500—more than a third—have returned to settle
in Israel. No record has been kept of returnees among the
students in the American Student Program, which has been
in operation now for more than a decade. The percentage
is doubtlessly much smaller, for reasons we have indicated,
but a number are now in Israel as settlers and others are potential immigrants.

The women students are more likely than the men to remain at the end of the year or to return to Israel after only
a brief span of time. They are less concerned than the men
with completing a full professional course of studies; and
in several cases, too, they became affianced to Israelis during their sojourn.

The Relative Weight of the "Jewish
Satisfaction"

The students who come back to settle in Israel do so, as
we have seen, because of some "unease" or dissatisfaction
with their lives as Jews in a non-Jewish environment and in
the expectation that they will find in Israel the corresponding satisfaction. Since the American settler has not "burned
his bridges," he may return at any time to the United
States. The chances are obviously greater that the student

who comes as an immigrant will remain—he has already had a taste of life in Israel. Even then he may experience deprivations which eventually outweigh in his eyes whatever satisfaction he does obtain. Features of Israeli life which hardly engaged his attention as visiting student now loom large for the settler. The kind of job he secures and the quality of the housing become matters of special concern. The new immigrant may suffer a great variety of frustrations ranging from minor irritations with bureaucratic procedures to major deprivations consequent on a reduced material standard of living. Whether he perseveres and overcomes them, or returns disillusioned to the States, would seem from our observations to depend in no small measure on whether in fact he experiences the Jewish satisfaction he sought, and what relative weight this satisfaction has in his life.

A number of the students who had returned as immigrants indicated that they strongly experienced this satisfaction (expressed with conviction in statements such as "here I feel at home—I belong," "I can live a complete Jewish life," "my children will grow up Jews") and were ready to forego material comforts and face up to difficulties in their new environment. Some of them add that in Israel they had captured the sense of being individuals making a meaningful contribution, not just anonymous cogs in a great machine. Such search for a purposeful role in society apparently complements the search for a more adequate sense of Jewish identity—or for an environmental context in which this identity can fully express itself.

The Immigrant and Social Contact

Returning with a time perspective which is no longer that of a temporary sojourner, the immigrant looks around

on the social plane for friendships of a more enduring kind.
A visiting student may view the lack of Israeli friends during his sojourn with exasperation or sorrow, but consoles himself with the thought that within measurable time he will be back among old friends in his home environment. For the immigrant friendships constitute the essential social core of what is now his permanent home. Israeli social circles are not easily penetrable, but the students returning as immigrants exert a more determined effort to enter them and report that in most cases they find congenial friends among other American settlers, and in the course of time among other Israelis as well.

The returning students believe that Israelis regard them with more respect—presumably without the ambivalence which previously characterized their attitude. They are no longer approached as desirable candidates for entry into the Israeli community who have to be challenged, cajoled, and even rebuked, but who in the final resort are unlikely to settle. At least one of the obstacles in the way of friendship between them and the Israelis no longer exists. A student who decided to settle and after a brief visit to his parents returned to Israel to continue his studies observes:

I would like to mention the vastly different, and to me surprising, reactions of those Israelis I had casually known in the hostel, when they saw me here the second year. For they had "pigeon-holed" me as a "one-yearer," and were visibly astonished to see me again.

And another student remarks in similar vein: "I am much more accepted as a fellow-resident. I am not one of those Americans leaving at the end of the year. People are prepared to take more trouble to form relationships."

As visiting students they had seen their Americanism as

constituting at times a barrier in the establishment of social relationships. They now find that in the course of daily living their Americanism places them at less of a disadvantage than they had anticipated, and that on occasion it is even an advantage.

I am not bothered any longer that I am looked upon as an American in Israel. It is done in an affectionate way—people are amused at my accent, at my mistakes in Hebrew. There are so many people who have come from other lands and I am no different in this respect.

Americans are wanted in Israel. The same cannot be said of a minority in the States.

In the interviews the students made no spontaneous references to discourtesy or unsociability on the part of Israelis. When they were specifically questioned on the subject, they tended to shrug it off as being no longer so important to them as once it was. Several of them took occasion to point to what they now saw as the positive side of Israeli roughedgedness—a bluntness and straightforwardness of manner. "It is true they are tactless. But it is not such a terribly negative quality. They say what they think. It is nice to be straight."

For some students Israeli "manners" still jar, albeit not too painfully. Their criticism loses some of its sharpness. At the same time they feel that since they are no longer just visitors they have more of a right to criticize. A student who had spoken of her continued dislike of "the shoving in line" adds: "I now feel freer in my criticisms. I am criticizing a part of myself."

In one area they were unsparing in their criticism. Some of them at the time of the interviews were still fresh as new immigrants from "a runaround," as they termed it, in Customs sheds, Government and Jewish Agency offices, and they minced no words in expressing their feelings about those responsible for this part of their experience.

The occupational role which a student usually enters when he settles constitutes an area of mutual interest with other Israelis; the meeting is no longer between an Israeli host and an American guest but between two residents of Israel sharing a common occupation and common problems. Two of our interviewees, who married Israelis and set up their homes in Jerusalem, described the meeting-ground they have with other housewives with whom they talk about the housekeeping problems they share. A student now at work in a Government office reported that he has had no difficulty in establishing friendships with the colleagues in the office with whom he is in daily contact. Students who return to embark on a professional course of studies at the Hebrew University find they establish contact on the basis of a mutuality of interests with their Israeli fellow-students in a way they could not do when they were visiting undergraduates pursuing general studies in the humanities or social sciences. A student at the Hebrew University's Paul Baerwald School of Social Work remembers that in the year she first came she would go from one large lecture room to another without establishing any friendly relations with the other students, and remarks contentedly: "Now, I am everyday with the same people and I am part of the class."

Students who have decided to settle tend to focus their attention on the positive facets of Israeli life which are consonant with this decision and in a sense justify it.[1] Thus, one of the student immigrants gave an enthusiastic account of how his views about the quality of life in Israel "skyrocketed," as he put it, from the moment he reached his decision.

The Problem of Language

The use of Hebrew is surrounded with more tension than before. It is now no longer an exercise in which success or failure is not crucial for any long-range future. A fluency in Hebrew is often necessary in the professions which the student immigrants usually enter; ignorance of the language imposes a limitation on their cultural and social life as well as on their professional activity. It takes considerable time and effort before the American immigrant can attain a proficiency in any way comparable to his fluency in English.

In the early stages the new immigrant may seek to use his limited Hebrew on every occasion, seeing in it a demonstration of his newly acquired Israeliness.[2] At times, however, he feels that his limited range of expression impoverishes his thought and that as he stumbles along in halting Hebrew he is really not his "old self." To make matters worse, the immigrant is often without the prestigious status he may have enjoyed in his country of origin and may be sorely in need of recognition. He now turns increasingly to English-speaking company for the support and the opportunities for self-expression it affords.

If this crisis in his adjustment is weathered and the immigrant feels his position in Israeli society more secure, he begins to use the two languages more freely in accordance with the demands of each particular situation.

The Impossibility of Complete "Assimilation"

Is the student now at long last an Israeli like all other Israelis, referring only to Israeli groups and their social norms, or is he still influenced by his American background? The conflict which took place during the sojourn is renewed when the student returns to Israel to settle. He discovers that, although he has thrown in his lot with Israel, a part of him is persistently American; his socialization for more than twenty years has been in an American culture and he cannot shed what he has acquired in this process. He cannot become an Israeli such as the native Israeli is. Gradually some of these new settlers begin to understand that complete "assimilation," or submersion of identity, is not possible, probably not even desirable. The settler begins to accept himself for what he is: an Israeli Jew with an American cultural background, the denial of which would be tantamount to a denial of self.[3] "If you are interested in shedding your Americanism, you are ashamed of what you are."

When the frustrations of life in a new country depress some of these settlers, they find solace in the thought that their children yet to be born will speak effortless Hebrew and will be more on the inside of life than they can ever be. There are some who go further and stoutly assert that the variegated composition of the Israeli community adds to the richness of its cultural life and that by virtue of their American training they have a specific contribution to make in a number of areas in which Israel is deficient. "It is a good thing more Americans are coming. We can give a lot to the culture."

CHAPTER 14

Problems and Perspectives

We have sought to view cross-cultural education within a series of conceptual contexts, in the belief that such a framework permits a systematic and meaningful organization of a multitude of seemingly disparate experiences. Although it was hoped in this way to lift our study beyond the plane of a narrow empirical investigation, we were aware of limitations of another character. We did not consider intragroup divergences produced by personality factors, nor could we properly explore the effect of differences in home, religious, and Jewish educational background. What we attempted to trace were the more common patterns in the reactions of a group of the kind we studied to certain facets of a sojourn experience.

These were students who came with favorable predispositions to a country in which they had a prior involvement, found in the experience of the sojourn confirmation of the favorable preconceptions, and, with few exceptions, returned to the home country with an enhanced sense of attachment to the country in which they had sojourned. Theirs was not merely a study sojourn; it also had something of the quality of a modern pilgrimage.

Implications for Planning

Some of our findings may be of pertinence in the planning of programs for other sojourns of this kind.

1. The enthusiasm evoked by the sojourn experience was tempered with some disappointment—in particular in the area of social contact with the hosts. This finding is not peculiar to our study; almost all studies of foreign students reflect a sense of dissatisfaction about social contact. The essence of the problem is not lack of goodwill on the part of the hosts. Even when goodwill prevails—as often it does—other factors produce the unsatisfactory social relationship. Among such factors are the cultural differences in acquaintanceship and friendship patterns and the absence of interests shared by the students and their hosts.

The problem of social contact does not admit of any easy solution, but if the expectations of the visitors are realistic, their disappointment is less intense. Thus, an explanation of the cultural differences—in orientation sessions at the start of the sojourn—can help the visiting students to understand the peculiarities of their hosts. The difficulties then do not arise unexpectedly and are borne more cheerfully when seen in proper perspective. Again, since the problem of social contact cannot be substantially alleviated by spurring the hosts on to acts of goodwill to the visitors, the emphasis should rather be on facilitating contacts between specific sectors of the host society and the visiting groups on the basis of a mutuality of interest.

2. An important role is played by what we have termed the "stranger group" in determining the adjustment and the attitudes of the students. It has some obvious disadvantages —the student can rest content with the companionship he finds within the group of fellow-strangers and is not compelled to venture beyond its confines into the host society. But, on the whole, these drawbacks seem outweighed by the advantages; the stranger group mitigates the loneliness which often overwhelms the solitary student in a strange

land and cushions him against other tribulations in the initial stages of adjustment. Any program for visiting students should take into account the potentialities of such a group which at many points mediates between the individual student and his new environment.

3. A visiting student obtains a deeper insight into the host society if he does not view it just from the outside but becomes a participant in some of its activities. Those students who volunteered to serve as teachers or counselors to immigrant youth were enthusiastic about the feeling this work gave them that they had become partners in the Israeli enterprise. The students were eager from the outset of their visit to move beyond the periphery of the host society, to cease to be just bystanders and to become participants. It is not always easy to organize this participation, but to the extent that it is feasible it adds greatly to the quality of the sojourn experience and to the involvement of the visiting students in the problems of their hosts.

4. Our students indicate that the primary purpose of their visit is to become acquainted with Israel not just as another foreign land but as a country which has a peculiar meaning for their lives as Jews. This purpose is substantially achieved, and they leave as Jews who have acquired a new inner staunchness. The study visit thus serves as an important complement to the education of a young American Jew.

5. Although the students return to the United States with a broadened conception of Jewishness and recognize the fact of Jewish interdependence, they nonetheless still lack a coherent, integrated conception of Jewish life in which Israel and the American Jewish community may be seen as interlocking parts of one Jewish world. In this area of Israel-Diaspora relationships confusion reigns; some clar-

ification of the issues could be attempted by initiating a dialogue on the subject with the students while they are in Israel.

6. Israel, which since the Six Day War is more anxious than ever to attract immigrants, hopes that many of the students will decide to settle in the country. The most likely such candidates for aliyah will be those students who attach importance to the Jewish component in their identity. Our study indicates that the motivation to settle stems primarily from what we have termed a "Jewish" factor, namely, from a feeling of unease or dissatisfaction as members of a Jewish minority in a non-Jewish majority culture and a search for a corresponding satisfaction in the Jewish majority society in Israel. It is this combination of "push" and "pull" which most often leads to immigration.

7. A note of caution to the hosts may be in place as to the manner in which they raise the subject of aliyah with the students during their sojourn. Israel is understandably interested in the students as potential settlers, but the visitors react adversely if they feel themselves unduly "pressurised" by their hosts. The sojourn should also not be planned by its organizers as just a passage-way to settlement in the country. It should continue to be broadly conceived as a study visit which allows the students, while pursuing their studies, to become more fully acquainted with Israel and the meaning it has for them. Such a sojourn experience, reinforced in recent years by the atmosphere of heightened morale and purposefulness prevailing in Israel, is bound to have a positive influence on the aliyah intentions of a number of students.

Many students, even if they have formed an intention to settle, will return to the United States to complete their studies. Whether the intention eventually becomes a decision will depend in no small measure on the establishment in the United States of appropriate social frameworks which will buttress whatever readiness the students developed during their sojourn to consider settlement. The decision to settle, as we have observed in an earlier chapter, is the culmination of a process which generally takes place in a group context.

Not only the intention to settle but other changes in attitudes produced by the sojourn require social support if they are to persist after the students return to their American environment.

8. The counselors, guides, and other personnel attached to groups of visiting students are the representatives of the host society with whom the students are in most frequent contact. The number of students visiting Israel is increasing at such a rate that special attention will have to be given to the training of a corps of Israeli madrichim qualified to work with overseas students.

Such training should give, among other things, an understanding of the psychological world of the American student and of the cultural differences which exist between him and his Israeli hosts. Americans who have settled in Israel are particularly suited to serve as counselors to visiting American students; the students, as we found, feel themselves closer to American settlers than to other Israelis and can turn to them more easily for advice because of the common background. Native Israelis also have a contribution to make as counselors but must first be sensitized to the needs of American students. Thus, although they understand the plight of a Jewry facing grave discrimination, they require to be given an insight—which a parallel study [1] of ours has shown many of them presently lack— into the subtler predicaments and dilemmas faced by Jews in the United States and other parts of the Western world, a sympathetic understanding of the Jewish unease and Jewish strivings peculiar to these communities.

9. When this study was nearing completion, a preliminary report of its tentative findings was discussed in orientation sessions with students freshly arrived in Israel. Presented as a piece of research, it was seen by the students as free of some of the "propagandistic" overtones often associated with orientation talks and was accordingly more readily accepted by them.

In the training of counselors and other personnel for work with overseas students yet another utilization of research seems desirable. These trainees should participate in a series of limited action-research projects in cross-cultural education; they will more readily accept the facts that they themselves discover about visiting students, their problems, and the process of re-education—these are now *"their facts"* and not simply the "facts" of a lecturer on the subject.[2]

The Changed Situation in the Two Countries

The group of students who were the principal subjects of this study visited Israel during the 1965–1966 academic year. The material was supplemented by the data obtained from a study conducted on a largely similar group who were in Israel during the 1966–1967 academic year. Although what we observed about the processes of cross-cultural education was confirmed as we moved from one group to the other, an important difference in the reactions to Israel appeared as a result of the Six Day War. The milieu in which the students sojourned underwent a sharp change during the months of May and June, 1967. They were now in a society with a renewed sense of purpose, increased cohesiveness, and an enhanced self-confidence. This society had become intensely interested in receiving more newcomers. These developments had a marked impact on the students, and although exact figures are not available, the indications are that the percentage who decided to remain in Israel at the conclusion of the year or to return to it in the near future far exceeded that of any previous year.

The American students in the 1967–1968, 1968–1969 academic years arrived in this different Israel with its soldiers standing on guard at Suez, on the Jordan, and on the Golan Heights. Their Israeli fellow-students were veterans of the Six Day War who had served an extended period of three years in the Army and were being called up from time to time for reserve duty (*milu'im*), reconciling themselves without complaint to further interruption of their studies, even on the eve of their examinations.

Two of their fellow-students from overseas, one from Uruguay and the other from South Africa, were killed by a bomb placed by terrorists in a Jerusalem supermarket; a number of them were present when an explosion occurred in the cafeteria in the Hebrew University library. A variety of guard duties were undertaken as part of the security measures in the face of terrorist attacks, and many overseas students volunteered for them. Similarly they were among the volunteers who aided in the work of frontier settlements exposed to bombardment by terrorists operating from Jordanian territory.

The students arriving during these years came to a sterner, and in a way a more impressive, reality than their predecessors of 1965 and 1966. Despite the fact that many Israeli students were still indifferent to social contact with the visitors (as shown by a survey carried out among the student population at the beginning of 1969 by the student newspaper, *Pi-Ha'aton*), the atmosphere in the country was such as to make the visiting students feel welcome and wanted.

Changes had taken place in their American environment as well. We have indicated in Chapter 12 that in the interviews conducted toward the end of 1968 a note of concern, at times even of disillusionment, about developments in the United States is discernible. Responses to questions addressed to American students in a psychology class at the Hebrew University in 1969 similarly reflected a growing pessimism. Thus, although the groups are not strictly comparable, it is of interest to note that the students in 1969 were more inclined than their 1965 predecessors to believe that antisemitism might become a serious menace in the United States (Table 67). The memory of the Holocaust also seems to have moved more strongly into their consciousness. Seventy-three per cent agreed with the statement that "Jews—wherever they be and even if they or their parents were never in Europe—should look upon themselves as if they are survivors of the Holocaust (the destruction of six million Jews in Europe)" (Table 68). Their comments about the lesson to be derived by Jews from this tragedy reflect more than in previous years a grim feeling of a continuing struggle for existence in which Jews are engaged.

Never again can we become complacent and ambivalent. We must look for and be ready and willing to fight. Antisemitism is in every place and level.

We must not let Hitler win posthumously, we must fight and survive thru Israel and Diaspora Jews working together.

The Jew is alone in the world. The only one that can help a Jew is a Jew. Everyone else just stands by.

Events in Israel and events in America had combined to give a new intensity to the Jewish identification of the students. The reasons given by the students in 1965 for their visit to Israel still prevail among the students in 1969, but they reveal a keener awareness of the relation of Israel to their Jewish identity and a more urgent search for the significance the sojourn in Israel may have for the further course of their lives in a world in turmoil.

Notes

Chapter 1. The Foreign Student

1. A comprehensive review of the research is given in Otto Klineberg, "Research in the Field of International Exchange in Education, Science and Culture," *Social Sciences Information*, IV (1965), 97–138. Klineberg sets out a number of key questions which require further research. Earlier reviews appear in H. Kelman (ed.), *International Behavior: A Social Psychological Analysis* (New York: Holt, Rinehart and Winston, 1965); S. O. Lesser and H. W. Peter, "Training Foreign Nationals in the United States," *Some Applications of Behavioral Research*, ed. R. Likert and S. P. Hayes (UNESCO, 1957), pp. 160–206; *Journal of Social Issues*, 1956, No. 1; 1962, No. 1; and 1963, No. 3; *International Social Science Bulletin*, 1955, No. 7; *Annals of the American Academy of Political and Social Science*, 1954, No. 295; C. Du Bois, *Foreign Students and Higher Education in the United States* (Washington: American Council on Education, 1956).

2. UNESCO, *Study Abroad*, XVII (Paris, 1968), 10. The following is the definition of a "student abroad" given in this publication: "A student abroad is a person who, after the completion of his secondary education, is studying at an institution of higher education in a country other than the one in which he has his permanent residence, and who has the intention (is not an immigrant) and the possibility (is not a refugee) of returning to his country of permanent residence after his studies" (XVI, 512).

3. The number of foreign students in the United States had

risen to 110,315 for the years 1967 to 1968. (Institute of International Education, *Open Doors* [New York, 1968]).

4. Institute of International Education, *Annual Report* (New York, 1965), p. 2.

5. For a discussion of evaluation procedures from the viewpoint of the administration of programs of international educational education, see A. J. A. Elliot, "The Evaluation of International Education: An Administrative Approach," *Social Sciences Information*, IV (1965), 61–78. See also Elliot, "Foreign Students in Perspective," *Social Science Information*, VI (1967), 189–202; and Klineberg.

6. One of the more comprehensive studies is by Robin M. Williams, Jr., *Strangers Next Door: Ethnic Relations in American Communities* (Englewood Cliffs, N.J.: Prentice-Hall, 1964).

7. For a pioneering study on the subject of social contact in cross-cultural education, see C. Selltiz et al., *Attitudes and Social Relations of Foreign Students in the United States* (Minneapolis: University of Minnesota Press, 1963).

8. F. D. Scott, *The American Experience of Swedish Students* (Minneapolis: University of Minnesota Press, 1956); R. L. Beals and N. D. Humphrey, *No Frontier to Learning: The Mexican Student in the United States* (Minneapolis: University of Minnesota Press, 1957); J. Watson and R. Lippitt, *Learning across Cultures: A Study of Germans Visiting America* (Ann Arbor: University of Michigan, 1955); J. W. Bennett, H. Passin, and R. K. McKnight, *In Search of Identity: The Japanese Overseas Scholar in America and Japan* (Minneapolis: University of Minnesota Press, 1958); G. V. Coelho, *Changing Images of America: A Study of Indian Students' Perceptions* (Glencoe, Ill.: Free Press, 1958); R. D. Lambert and M. Bressler, *Indian Students on an American Campus* (Minneapolis: University of Minnesota Press, 1956); John Useem and Ruth Useem, *The Western-Educated Man in India: A Study of His Social Roles and Influence* (New York: Dryden Press, 1955); W. Sewell and O. Davidsen, *Scandinavian Students on an American Campus* (Minneapolis: Univer-

sity of Minnesota Press, 1961). In their study, John and Ruth Useem compare Indian students who have studied in Britain with those who have studied in the United States. For another study of students in Britain see *Colonial Students in Britain,* a report by PEP (Political and Economic Planning) (London, 1955). Further studies of foreign students in countries other than the United States are referred to in Klineberg.

9. J. T. Gullahorn and J. E. Gullahorn, "An Extension of the U-Curve Hypothesis," *Journal of Social Issues,* XIX (1963), 33–47; I. de Sola Pool, "Effects of Cross-National Contact on National and International Images" in Kelman, pp. 106–129. Cf. studies of Peace Corps volunteers, such as the following: M. I. Stein, *Volunteers for Peace: The First Group of Peace Corps Volunteers in a Rural Community Development Program in Colombia, South America* (New York: Wiley, 1965); and M. B. Smith et al., "A Factorial Study of Morale among Peace Corps Teachers in Ghana," *Journal of Social Issues,* XIX (1963), 10–32.

Cf. R. D. Lambert and M. Bressler, "The Sensitive-area Complex: A Contribution to the Theory of Guided Culture Contact," *American Journal of Sociology,* LX (1955), 583–592.

11. Bennett et al.

12. R. T. Morris: *The Two-Way Mirror: National Status in Foreign Students' Adjustment* (Minneapolis: University of Minnesota Press, 1960).

13. The problem of the nonreturnees is discussed by Klineberg, pp. 108–109. See also W. Adams (ed.), *The Brain Drain* (New York: Macmillan, 1968). Israel faces a similar problem; a number of Israeli students who proceed for study abroad do not return.

Chapter 2. The Psychological Field of the Foreign Student

1. Our analysis is in terms of Lewinian field theory. Cf. the analysis of the adolescent's situation in Kurt Lewin, *Field*

Theory in Social Science (New York: Harper, 1951), pp. 135–145.

2. S. Lysgaard, "Adjustment in a Foreign Society: Norwegian Fulbright Grantees Visiting the United States," *International Social Science Bulletin*, VII (1955), 45–51.

3. S. Schachter, *The Psychology of Affiliation* (Stanford, Calif.: Stanford University Press, 1959). Cf. the functions of college peer groups, in T. M. Newcomb and E. K. Wilson (eds.), *College Peer Groups* (Chicago: Aldine, 1966). Cf. also the behavior of immigrants in a new situation, in L. Fuchs, *The Political Behavior of American Jews* (Glencoe, Ill.: Free Press, 1956): "Lacking information and experience in American politics, often unable to speak English, immigrants gave special weight to advice given to them by one of their own kind in their own language" (p. 15).

4. A stimulating discussion of the position of the stranger is provided by Simmel in *The Sociology of Georg Simmel,* ed. K. H. Wolff (Glencoe, Ill.: Free Press, 1950), pp. 403–408. See also A. Schuetz, "The Stranger: An Essay in Social Psychology," *American Journal of Sociology*, XLIX (1944), 499–507.

5. Problems relating to the "visibility" of norms are discussed by R. K. Merton, *Social Theory and Social Structure* (Glencoe, Ill.: Free Press, 1957), pp. 336–353.

6. K. Lewin, "Some Differences between the United States and Germany," *Resolving Social Conflicts* (New York: Harper, 1948), p. 18.

7. L. M. Killian, "The Significance of Multiple-Group Membership in Disaster," *American Journal of Sociology*, LVII (1952), 309–314.

8. J. R. P. French and R. B. Zajonc, "An Experimental Study of Cross-Cultural Norm Conflict," *Journal of Abnormal and Social Psychology*, LIV (1957), 218–224.

9. R. G. Barker et al., "Adjustment to Physical Handicap and Illness," *Social Science Research Council Bulletin*, No. 55 (1953), pp. 39–42.

10. For an analysis of salience and valence as the determinants of relative potency, see S. N. Herman and E. O. Schild, "Ethnic Role Conflict in a Cross-Cultural Situation," *Human Relations*, XIII (1960), 215–228.

11. H. H. Kelley, "Salience of Membership and Resistance to Change of Group-Anchored Attitudes," *Human Relations*, VIII (1955), 275–289. W. W. Charters and T. M. Newcomb, "Some Attitudinal Effects of Experimentally Increased Salience of a Membership Group," *Readings in Social Psychology*, ed. E. E. Maccoby, T. M. Newcomb, and E. L. Hartley (3d ed.; New York: Holt, 1958), pp. 276–281. W. E. Lambert et al., "The Effect of Increased Salience of a Membership Group on Pain Tolerance," *Journal of Personality*, XXVIII (1960), 350–357.

12. Charters and Newcomb.

13. In treating problems of change in the cross-cultural situation in terms of changing salience a link is established with studies in the field of perception. An example of the possibilities inherent in this link is provided by a study by J. S. Bruner and H. V. Perlmutter, "Compatriot and Foreigner: A Study of Impression Formation in Three Countries," *Journal of Abnormal and Social Psychology*, LV (1957), 253–260.

14. Cf. Kelley.

15. Social research is beginning to give more attention to problems of time perspective. Among the early theoretical statements are those by L. K. Frank, "Time Perspectives," *Journal of Social Philosophy*, IV (1939), 293–312; and K. Lewin, *Field Theory in Social Science*.

16. Cf. M. Jahoda, "Conformity and Independence: A Psychological Analysis," *Human Relations*, XII (1960), 99–119. "When the time dimension of the life space is balanced between past, present and future, independent action is most likely" (p. 117).

17. Cf. R. Kastenbaum, "The Structure and Function of Time Perspective," *Journal of Psychological Researches*, VIII (1964), 1–11. The dimensions of time perspective designated

by Kastenbaum as "extension," "coherence," and "density" correspond to what we call "scope," "structure," and "differentiation." What he terms "directionality" or "movement" has elements in common with the "past-present-future orientation," under which we subsume the "controllability of locomotion."

18. R. Barker, T. Dembo, and K. Lewin, *Frustration and Regression: An Experiment with Young Children*, Studies in Topological and Vector Psychology, II (Iowa City: University of Iowa Press, 1941).

19. Cf. Lewin, "Time Perspective and Morale," *Resolving Social Conflicts*, pp. 103–124.

20. E. H. Erikson, "Ego Identity and the Psychosocial Moratorium," *New Perspectives for Research on Juvenile Delinquency*, ed. H. L. Witner and R. Kotinsky (Washington D.C.: U.S. Govt. Printing Office, 1955), pp. 1–23.

Chapter 3. Background and Methods of Study

1. The junior year is generally regarded as a convenient stage at which to proceed for study abroad. The two years at the American college have provided the student with a foundation for his academic program, and after the junior year abroad he returns for the senior year which he completes at his American college.

2. The proportion of students from the religious movements varies from year to year. In 1965, eleven declared themselves to be Orthodox, 24 Conservative, 15 Reform, and 24 nonreligious. Five did not indicate with which of the religious groups they were affiliated.

3. Like most studies of cross-cultural education, ours is a nonexperimental field study. (A rare exception is the work by French and Zajonc, "An Experimental Study of Cross-Cultural Norm Conflict," *Journal of Abnormal and Social Psychology*, LIV [1957].) Our study differs from most of the others in some ways: the students were questioned not only during the

sojourn, but also before their arrival and after their return home; we were able to observe a succession of closely similar groups undergoing the experience of the sojourn in the same setting.

The students we studied were at a developmental stage in their lives when there are many vagaries in attitudes. Unfortunately it was not feasible to set up a control group of their peers in the United States.

4. The group included 87 students, but not all came by ship. The first questionnaire was completed by the 79 students who were on the ship. We did not succeed in reaching all students with our questionnaire in Israel, and the *n* for the second questionnaire was 73.

5. We cannot rule out the possibility of a selective factor in the return of the questionnaires, but our comparison in any case is limited to 29 students who responded both to the second questionnaire in Israel and to the questionnaire circulated in the United States.

6. C. E. Osgood, G. J. Suci, and P. H. Tannenbaum, *The Measurement of Meaning* (Urbana: University of Illinois Press, 1957).

7. We cannot tell whether these respondents to the mailed questionnaire are representative of the entire group of students who had visited Israel during the years 1965–1968. We shall accordingly analyze their responses as indicators of trends appearing among this limited sector without generalizing beyond it.

Chapter 4. Israeli Hosts and Their Student Guests: Communalities and Differences

1. We are using the term "ethnic" in a broad sense similar to that in which Otto Klineberg employs it: "An ethnic group may be defined . . . as one which is set off from others by inherited physical type (or 'race'), by religion, language, or national orgin, or any combination of these" ("The Multi-

National Society: Some Research Problems," *Social Sciences Information*, VI [1967], 84).

2. S. N. Herman, *Israelis and Jews: A Study in the Continuity of an Identity* (New York: Random House, forthcoming). The study encompassed (1) a representative sample of eleventh graders (16–17 year age level) in Israel's schools (2) the parents of a subsample of the pupils, and (3) the teachers of relevant subjects in the schools falling within the sample.

3. Cf. the study by I. L. Child of second-generation Italians in the United States, *Italian or American? The Second Generation in Conflict* (New Haven: Yale University Press, 1943): "the individual of the second generation acquires habits and attitudes that conform to two cultures, and it has been seen that these two cultures differ at many points" (p. 49).

4. Cf. the analysis by Isidor Chein, "The Problem of Jewish Identification," *Jewish Social Studies*, XVII (1955), 219–222. "A competitive situation thus develops and one can do (think, or feel) something Jewish only by giving up or withdrawing from something in the stream of general activities."

5. The students will, however, encounter two very small extremist groups who see an incompatibility between feeling Jewish and feeling Israeli. The one group, Naturei Karta ("Guardians of the Walls"), regard themselves as Jews only and look upon the establishment of a State of Israel by secular forces as a profane act. The other group (called "Canaanites") regard themselves as Israelis only and wish to disassociate themselves from a Jewish people and a Jewish past.

6. The nature of the relationship between Israeliness and Jewishness is often not adequately comprehended by visitors to Israel. So insightful an observer as Georges Friedmann, *The End of the Jewish People?* (New York: Doubleday, 1967), underestimates the extent to which Israeliness and Jewishness are interwoven.

7. Herman. After the Six Day War the marking-off function of the Arab minority may have increased.

8. *Ibid.*

9. Cf. the excellent study of an American Jewish community by Marshall Sklare and Joseph Greenblum, *Jewish Identity on the Suburban Frontier: A Study of Group Survival in the Open Society*, The Lakeville Studies, I (New York: Basic Books, 1967). The authors discuss "the meager Jewishness to which the Lakeville youngster falls heir" (p. 331).

10. Herman.

Chapter 5. In the New Situation: The Unfamiliar Homeland

1. In the study of Israeli high-school pupils (S. N. Herman, *Israelis and Jews: A Study in the Continuity of an Identity* [New York: Random House, forthcoming].) 25 per cent of the sample classified themselves as "dati'im" (orthodoxly religious), 32 per cent as "mesorati'im" (traditionalists), and 42 per cent as "lo dati'im" (nonreligious)—with 1 per cent unclassified. The terms relate to degrees of religious *observance*. "Dati" implies a strict observance of religious obligations; "mesorati" indicates a positive orientation to Jewish tradition accompanied by varying degrees of laxity and selectivity about observance; "lo dati" means nonobservant (although here too some customs may be honored).

The percentage of orthodoxly religious youth in the population at large would be appreciably higher than the 25 per cent indicated by the sample. The sample is of the high-school population, and at this level the Oriental communities, who are less secularized than the Ashkenazic sector, are underrepresented. The religious distribution of youngsters from the Oriental communities in the sample was as follows: "dati'im" 34 per cent; "mesorati'im" 44 per cent; "lo dati'im" 22 per cent. The sample furthermore did not include the comparatively small number of ultra-orthodox pupils at schools not within the framework of the Ministry of Education.

2. Cf. S. N. Herman, "Explorations in the Social Psychology of Language Choice," *Human Relations*, XIV (1961), 149–164. "Speaking an unfamiliar language is equivalent to entering into a new psychological situation. Directions are uncertain—the improper use of an idiomatic phrase, for example, may hold the speaker up to derision. He feels himself on unstable ground" (p. 156).

3. Conceivably some "attitudinal aggression" engendered by the frustrations arising from the encounter with Israelis may also be directed against the language. Cf. R. B. Zajonc, "Aggressive Attitudes of the Stranger as a Function of Conformity Pressures," *Human Relations*, V (1952), 205–216.

Chapter 6. Strangers among Kinsfolk: The Problem of Social Contact

1. This feeling of kinship may even be experienced by a Jew hitherto distant from the center of the Jewish group. Thus, Georges Friedmann in *The End of the Jewish People?* (New York: Doubleday, 1967) observes: "Why did I feel I was among close relations when I saw boys and girls lying about on the grass of the campus of the Hebrew University, their books at their feet, talking in the sunshine of a precocious spring, their eyes sometimes exchanging the message of an approaching idyll?" (p. 13).

2. "Some Factors Which Influence the Attitudinal Outcomes of Personal Contact," *International Social Science Bulletin*, VII (1955), 51–58.

3. Cf. the analysis by Kurt Lewin of social psychological differences between the United States and Germany in *Resolving Social Conflicts* (New York: Harper, 1948), pp. 3–33.

4. R. K. Merton, basing himself on Georg Simmel, provides

a stimulating discussion of the "openness" and "completeness" of groups in his *Social Theory and Social Structure*
(Glencoe, Ill.: Free Press, 1957). "Just as individuals differ in
aspirations to affiliate themselves with particular groups, so do
groups differ in their concern to enlarge or to restrict their
membership. This is to say that groups, and social structures
generally, may be relatively open or closed" (p. 292). "The
property of completeness, isolated by Simmel but largely ignored by sociologists since his day, refers to the ratio of actual
members of a group or organization to its potential members,
i.e., to those who satisfy the operative criteria for membership"
(p. 314).

5. J. E. Hofman and I. Zak, "Interpersonal Contact and
Attitude Change in a Cross-Cultural Situation," *Journal of
Social Psychology*, LXXVIII (1969), 165–171.

6. Cf. D. Cartwright, "Achieving Change in People," *Human Relations*, IV (1951), 381–392.

Chapter 7. In Overlapping Situations: The Changing Salience of an Ethnic Role

1. J. S. Bruner and H. V. Perlmutter, "Compatriot and
Foreigner: A Study of Impression Formation in Three Coun-
ties," *Journal of Abnormal and Social Psychology*, LV (1957):
"Our first and most general hypothesis is that if objects that
are alike in all respects, save one, are considered *together*,
their difference in this one respect will be more critical in the
impression one forms of the objects. . . . A corollary of this
hypothesis to which we have addressed ourselves is: If in forming impressions of foreigners and compatriots one is thinking
in a comparative context, with the differing nationalities in
mind while forming one's impression, then the degree to which
nationality will influence the impressions formed will be increased" (p. 259).

2. It would have been interesting in this connection to test

Notes

the reactions of the Israeli students when confronted with two groups of visiting students, one Jewish and the other non-Jewish.

3. E. H. Erikson, *Childhood and Society* (New York: Norton, 1950), p. 213.

4. S. A. Stouffer, "An Analysis of Conflicting Social Norms," *American Sociological Review*, XIV (1949), 707.

5. S. N. Herman and E. O. Schild, "Ethnic Role Conflict in a Cross-Cultural Situation," *Human Relations*, XIII (1960), 215–228.

Chapter 8. The Time Perspective of the Sojourner

1. For a review of the studies and a discussion of the implications of the U-curve, see O. Klineberg, "Research in the Field of International Exchanges in Education, Science and Culture," *Social Sciences Information*, IV (1965), 105–108. See also S. O. Lesser and H. W. Peter, "Training Foreign Nationals in the United States," *Some Applications of Behavioral Research*, ed. R. Likert and S. P. Hayes (UNESCO, 1957), pp. 160–206. Eugene Jacobson suggests a nine-phase sequence in his paper, "Sojourn Research: A Definition of the Field," *Journal of Social Issues*, XIX (1963), 123–129.

2. The term "engagement" in this context has a more restricted meaning appropriate to the description of this phase of the sojourn.

3. This question was asked at the end of the seventh month of the stay. Our impression was that in the ensuing months there was a further improvement in mood. The interviews conducted toward the end of the stay revealed considerable satisfaction on the part of the students with their sojourn experience.

4. Kurt Lewin has discussed what a historical time perspective meant to the Zionists in Germany under the Nazi regime in his essay, "Time Perspective and Morale" in *Resolving Social Conflicts* (New York: Harper, 1948): "They

had a time perspective which included a psychological past of surviving adverse conditions for thousands of years and a meaningful and inspiring goal for the future. As the result of such a time perspective, this group showed high morale—despite a present which was judged by them to be no less foreboding than by others" (p. 104). Cf. also a discussion on the role of ideology in the adjustment of immigrants from Europe with a Zionist background by J. T. Shuval, *Immigrants on the Threshold* (New York: Atherton Press, 1963). "European Zionists are less disappointed with Israel than European non-Zionists . . . the ideology of the Europeans apparently provided some sort of frame of reference for experiences in Israel so that it was possible for the European immigrants to balance disappointments against remote and valued goals rather than against immediate frustrations" (p. 76).

5. S. N. Herman, *Israelis and Jews: A Study in the Continuity of an Identity* (New York: Random House, forthcoming).

6. For a discussion of time perspective as a component of "involvement" see S. N. Herman, Y. Peres, and E. Yuchtman, "Reactions to the Eichmann Trial in Israel: A Study in High Involvement," *Scripta Hierosolymitana*, XIV (The Hebrew University, Jerusalem: Magnes Press, 1965), 98–118.

Chapter 9. The Intention to Settle: The "Push" and the "Pull"

1. Cf. K. Lewin, *Field Theory in Social Science* (New York: Harper, 1951): "The strength of the force toward or away from a valence depends upon the strength of that valence and the psychological distance between the person and the valence" (p. 258).

2. Cf. the analysis of the motivation to migrate by S. N. Eisenstadt, *The Absorption of Immigrants* (London: Routledge, 1954): "We assume that every migratory movement is motivated by the migrant's feeling of some kind of insecurity

Notes

and inadequacy in his original social setting" (p. 1). See also
C. Wright Mills, C. Senior, and R. K. Goldsen, *The Puerto
Rican Journey* (New York: Harper, 1950); and P. H. Rossi,
"Why Families Move," *The Language of Social Research*, ed.
P. F. Lazarsfeld, and M. Rosenberg (Glencoe, Ill.: Free Press,
1955), pp. 457–468. In a paper, "English Migrants to New
Zealand: The Decision to Move," *Human Relations*, XIII
(1960) 167–174, L. B. Brown observes that "the relationship
between the pushes and pulls is complex, with each of these
forces interacting and having both positive and negative components" (p. 168).

3. C. H. Stember et al., *Jews in the Mind of America* (New
York: Basic Books, 1966), summarize the findings of public
polls over a period of twenty-five years from 1937 onward.
Their conclusion (which relates to the position before 1966)
is that "anti-Jewish prejudice obviously is not yet a thing of
the past, any more than anti-Jewish discrimination is, but
both are unmistakably in a state of decline" (p. 217). The
implications of this observation are debated by several of the
contributors to the volume.

4. See the paper (in Hebrew) by S. N. Herman, "Mesilot
la-Ziyonut he-Haluzit" ["Pathways to Chalutzic Zionism"],
in *Ha-Ziyonut be-Sha'a zu* [*Zionism in the Contemporary
Period*], ed. G. Hanoch (Jerusalem: Zionist Organization,
1951), pp. 131–137.

5. The "push" may also be due to idiosyncratic factors in
the background of the particular student or conceivably to a
distaste for general features of American society which do not
relate directly to majority-minority relations. In the group we
studied, however, it was unease about their position as members of a Jewish minority group which stood out as the dominant factor in the "push."

6. $\gamma = 0.35$. For the use of *gamma* (γ) as a measure of association, see H. L. Conster, "Criteria for Measures of Association," *American Sociological Review*, XXX (1965),
341–352.

Notes

7. $\gamma = 0.64$.
8. Cf. Eli Ginzberg, *Occupational Choice* (New York: Columbia University Press, 1951).
9. See Merton et al., *The Student Physician* (Cambridge, Mass.: Harvard University Press, 1957), for discussion of the protracted process leading to a student's decision to study Medicine. The authors also discuss how the social context affects the degree of stress attending the decision to specialize in one branch of medicine rather than another: "The student who decides to specialize in psychiatry in one school, where great value is attached to this field, will be in a substantially different social and psychological situation than the *same kind* of student making this decision in another school in which psychiatry is often derogated. This may serve, if only by way of tentative illusion, to suggest that the same career decisions will have differing psychological significance depending upon the social context" (p. 71).
10. K. Lewin, "Intention, Will and Need," *Organization and Pathology of Thought,* ed. D. Rapaport (New York: Columbia University Press, 1951): "When in a person there are several, simultaneous tension-systems of opposing directions, a decision often amounts to the effecting of some kind of equilibrium among them, or to isolating some of them. At any rate, the internal situation created is one in which a more or less unitary tension-system controls the action. Occasionally in such cases, an internal vacillation is observed before the decision (the so-called struggle of motives)" (p. 137).
11. Lewin, *Field Theory in Social Science*: "The forces toward a positive, or away from a negative, valence can be called 'driving' forces. They lead to locomotion. These locomotions might be hindered by physical or social obstacles. Such barriers correspond to 'restraining' forces. Restraining forces, as such, do not lead to locomotion, but they do influence the effect of driving forces" (p. 259).

Chapter 10. Effects of the Sojourn

1. Among the more penetrating analyses of the process of change are: K. Lewin, "Conduct, Knowledge and the Acceptance of New Values," *Resolving Social Conflicts* (New York: Harper, 1948), pp. 56–68; and D. Cartwright, "Achieving Change in People," *Human Relations*, IV (1951), 381–392.

2. An insightful description of what a visit to Israel means to even a "peripheral" or "marginal" Jew is given by Georges Friedmann in *The End of the Jewish People?* (New York: Doubleday, 1967): "Visiting Israel is certainly a disturbing experience to any Jew, however peripheral or marginal a Jew he may be. It may rouse his enthusiasm or irritate him, but it will certainly shake him" (p. 13). The impact of Israel was all the more marked on students coming with ardent feelings for the country.

3. K. Lewin, *Field Theory in Social Science* (New York: Harper, 1951), pp. 145–148.

4. $\gamma = 0.28$.

5. Cf. L. Berkowitz and L. R. Daniels, "Affecting the Salience of the Social Responsibility Norm: Effects of Past Help on the Response to Dependency Relationships," *Journal of Abnormal and Social Psychology*, LXVIII (1964), 275–281.

6. The favorableness of an adjective in any of the pairs was determined by its rating for "myself as I would like to be." The overall favorableness of a concept was determined by calculating the mean of the ratings on the 15 adjective pairs appearing at the top of the list on Table 49. In regard to these adjectives, a clear indication was available as to which member of the pair had the favorable connotation, i.e., which had received a mean score of 6 and above for "myself as I would like to be." Adjectives about which such high consensus did not exist were excluded. Furthermore, the four adjectives dealing with pride in Americanism, Israeliness, Jewishness, and roots in Jewishness, were not included in the comparison since they were not common to all the concepts.

7. Cf. Friedmann: "Israel also forces the Jewish observer, in spite of all his reticence, to ask himself what his Jewishness is and what it means to him" (p. 14).

8. R. W. White, *Lives in Progress* (New York: Dryden Press, 1952), p. 338.

9. Cf. C. Wagley and M. Harris, *Minorities in the New World* (N.Y.: Columbia University Press, 1958): "Jewish affiliation, whether it involves merely being born of Jewish parents or adherence to one of the various forms of the Jewish religion, is a stigma and in one way or another it acts as a brake on upward social and economic mobility" (p. 204). Cf. also E. Goffman, *Stigma: Notes on the Management of Spoiled Identity* (Englewood Cliffs, N.J.: Prentice-Hall, 1963).

10. Cf. Marian Radke Yarrow, "Personality Development and Minority Group Membership," *The Jews: Social Patterns of an American Group*, ed. M. Sklare (Glencoe, Ill.: Free Press, 1957), pp. 451–474.

11. Joan and Esther were members of the panel group. We have grafted on to the material supplied by John quotations from the interviews with two other students occupying an ideological position similar to his. The profile of John should therefore be regarded as a composite.

Chapter 11. The Students and the Six Day War: In Face of a Common Danger

1. For an exposition of some of the consequences of decisions see L. Festinger, *A Theory of Cognitive Dissonance* (Evanston, Ill.: Row, Peterson, 1957).

Chapter 13. The Student as an Immigrant

1. "Postdecision dissonance may be reduced by increasing the attractiveness of the chosen alternative, decreasing the attractiveness of the unchosen alternatives, or both" (L. Festinger, *A Theory of Cognitive Dissonance* [Evanston, Ill.: Row, Peterson, 1957], p. 264).

2. For an analysis of the developmental pattern in the use of Hebrew and English by a new immigrant, see S. N. Herman, "Explorations in the Social Psychology of Language Choice," *Human Relations*, IV (1961), 149–164.

3. Cf. T. Parsons, "The Position of Identity in the General Theory of Action," *The Self in Social Interaction*, ed. C. Gordon and K. J. Gergen, I (New York: Wiley, 1968), 11–23: "Being an American living in the mid-twentieth century is *constitutive* of my identity. If, for example, I should 'defect' to Communist China, I would always remain to myself and others 'that American who defected,' or 'became converted,' according to the perspective. I could never have the identity of Chinese Communist without the 'American' understratum, unless I had been born and brought up entirely within the Chinese Communist system" (p. 21).

Chapter 14. Problems and Perspectives

1. S. N. Herman, *Israelis and Jews: A Study in the Continuity of an Identity* (New York: Random House, forthcoming).

2. A. J. Marrow and J. R. P. French, Jr., "Changing a Stereotype in Industry," *Journal of Social Issues*, I (1945), 33–37; I. Chein, S. W. Cook, and J. Harding, "The Field of Action Research," *American Psychologist*, III (1948), 43–50.

Tables

Tables relate to the 1965–1966 American Student Program, unless otherwise indicated. Those tables which are based on the responses of the 1966–1967 group are tables numbered 8, 10, 14, 15, 16, 20, 25, 26, 28, 57, 58. Tables 29 and 30, as indicated, relate to an earlier study carried out at the Leadership Institute in Jerusalem. A few tables—numbers 3, 4, 13, 23—from studies of Israeli high school students have been added for comparative purposes; an appropriate indication is given in each case.

In tables comparing the students' responses to the first questionnaire with those to the questionnaire completed toward the end of the sojourn, an asterisk before the heading indicates that the difference in the responses is statistically significant (according to the Sign Test).

The n for the 1965–1966 A.S.P. group varies between 79 and 73. The n for the 1966–1967 group is 83. The responses of these groups are given in percentages. Where the tables refer to smaller groups, the numbers are indicated in addition to the percentages.

1. American-Jewish: overlap and consonance as perceived by the students (in per cent; $n = 79$)

When I feel more American I also feel more Jewish	14
There is no relationship between my feeling Jewish and my feeling American	68
I feel less Jewish	18

Tables

2. Jewish-American: overlap and consonance as perceived by the students (in per cent; $n = 79$)

When I feel more Jewish
I also feel more American   13
There is no relationship between my feeling Jewish and my
    feeling American   61
I feel less American   26

---

3. Israeli-Jewish: overlap and consonance as perceived by Israeli high-school students (in per cent; $n = 2,980$)

When I feel more Israeli
I also feel more Jewish   67
There is no relationship between my feeling Jewish and my
    feeling Israeli   29
I feel less Jewish   4

---

4. Jewish-Israeli: overlap and consonance as perceived by Israeli high-school students (in per cent; $n = 2,980$)

When I feel more Jewish
I also feel more Israeli   70
There is no relationship between my feeling Jewish and my
    feeling Israeli   27
I feel less Israeli   3

---

5. Valence of Jewishness (in per cent; $n = 79$)

If you were to be born all over again, would you wish to be born a Jew?
1. I would very much wish to be born a Jew   65
2. I would wish to be born a Jew   22
3. I would not mind whether I was born a Jew or not   11
4. I would prefer not to be born a Jew   0
    Median $= 1.25$

---

6. Valence of United States (in per cent; $n = 79$)

If you were to be born all over again, would you wish to be born in the United States?
1. I would very much wish to be born in the U.S.   39
2. I would wish to be born in the U.S.   31

3. I would not mind being born in another country   24
4. I would prefer to be born in another country   6
     Median = 1.85

---

7. The Jewish-American continuum (in per cent; $n = 78$)

Below is a rating scale, at one end of which appears the word "Jewish" and at the other end the word "American." Indicate your position on this scale by placing a checkmark X within the appropriate compartment on this scale. To the extent that the mark is near to "American" it means that you feel yourself so much more American than Jewish. To the extent that the mark X is nearer to "Jewish" it means that you feel yourself so much more Jewish. Please note that the mark X should be placed inside the space between the points on the scale.

American : 7 : 6 : 5 : 4 : 3 : 2 : 1 : Jewish

<u>17</u>   <u>48</u>

American : 0 : 5 : 12 : 35 : 24 : 14 : 10 : Jewish

Median = 3.55

---

8. Closeness to groups in Israel, 1966–1967 A.S.P. (in per cent; $n = 83$)

How close do you feel toward the following groups?

Groups	Very close	Close	Not so close	Not close at all	No reply	Median
Israeli students	4	17	57	10	13	2.9
The A.S.P. students	36	47	12	0	5	1.7
Veteran American settlers in Israel	13	40	29	10	8	2.3
Veteran Eastern European settlers in Israel	7	29	39	20	5	2.9
New immigrants from the Oriental countries	5	22	31	34	8	3.1
New immigrants from the European countries	4	19	41	28	8	3.1
Sabras	5	18	54	13	10	2.9

* 9. Attitude toward Hebrew (in per cent)

How do you feel about Hebrew?	Before arrival ($n = 97$)	After sojourn ($n = 73$)
I have very positive feelings about it	65	53
I have positive feelings about it	33	38
I have no special feeling about it	1	8
I have negative feelings about it	1	0
I have very negative feelings about it	0	0
Median	1.27	1.43
$p < .05$		

10. Salience of Jewishness, 1966–1967 A.S.P. (in per cent; $n = 83$)

Where did you have more occasion to think of yourself as a Jew?	
1. Very much more often in the U.S.	16
2. More often in the U.S.	22
3. About equally in Israel and the U.S.	28
4. More often in Israel	25
5. Very much more often in Israel	6
6. No reply	3
Median = 2.87	

11. Role in which students prefer to be seen (in per cent; $n = 79$)

When you come to Israel how would you like the Israelis to see you?	
First and foremost as a Jew	76
First and foremost as an American	10
Other replies	8
No reply	6

12. Role in which students believe they are seen (in per cent; $n = 73$)

How do you think the Israelis see you?	
First and foremost as a Jew	13
First and foremost as an American	86
Other replies	1

13. Perception of American Jewish students by Israeli students (in per cent; $n = 78$)

How do you see the American Jewish students studying at the University?
First and foremost as Americans   40
First and foremost as Jews   60

---

14. Role in which Israelis are perceived, 1966–1967 A.S.P. (in per cent; $n = 83$)

How do you in fact see the Israelis?
First and foremost as Jews   23
First and foremost as Israelis   73
No reply   4

---

15. Role in which students would have preferred to perceive Israelis, 1966–1967 A.S.P. (in per cent; $n = 83$)

How would you have preferred to see the Israelis?
First and foremost as Jews   59
First and foremost as Israelis   25
No reply   16

---

16. Salience of Americanism, 1966–1967 A.S.P. (in per cent; $n = 83$)

Where did you have more occasion to think of yourself as an American?
1. Very much more often in the U.S.   1
2. More often in the U.S.   3
3. About equally in Israel and the U.S.   16
4. More often in Israel   43
5. Very much more often in Israel   36
   No reply   1
      Median = 4.20

---

17. Pride in being a Jew / in being an American $(n = 39)$

At the end of your year's stay, do you feel any change whatsoever in your sense of pride in being a Jew / in being an American?

	In being a Jew		In being an American	
	%	n	%	n
More proud	61	24	26	10
Less proud	9	3	20	8
No change	30	12	43	17
Other replies	0	0	11	4

18. Strength of feeling of being Jewish (in per cent)

Below is a rating scale, one end of which indicates the position of a person with a strong feeling of being Jewish and the other end a person with no feeling of being Jewish. Indicate your position on this scale by placing a checkmark X within the appropriate compartment on this scale.

A person with a strong feeling of being Jewish	: 7 : 6 : 5 : 4 : 3 : 2 : 1 :	A person with no feeling of being Jewish
Before arrival $(n = 79)$	: 48 : 37 : 8 : 1 : 4 : 1 : 1 :	Median = 6.43
After sojourn $(n = 73)$	: 49 : 26 : 10 : 11 : 1 : 3 : 0 :	Median = 6.46

* 19. Strength of feeling of being American (in per cent)

In the same way check your position on the following scale.

A person with a strong feeling of being American	: 7 : 6 : 5 : 4 : 3 : 2 : 1 :	A person with no feeling of being American
Before arrival $(n = 79)$	: 27 : 23 : 15 : 15 : 6 : 14 : 0 :	Median = 5.50
After sojourn $(n = 73)$	: 29 : 37 : 7 : 10 : 1 : 16 : 0 :	Median = 5.93

$p < .05$

20. Relative salience, valence and potency of ethnic role across situations, 1966–1967 A.S.P. (in per cent; $n = 83$)

During your stay in Israel there are situations in which you may see yourself primarily as Jewish, in some primarily as American, in some primarily as a resident of Israel. How do you think you would see yourself in the following situations, how do you think those you are in contact with see you, and how would you like them to see you?

Situation	Ethnic role	I see myself primarily as	They see me primarily as	I would like them to see me primarily as
In contact with Israeli students	Jewish	9	1	29
	American	72	92	19
	Res. of Israel	12	0	40
	No reply	7	7	12
In correspondence with Jewish friends in America	Jewish	30	29	35
	American	21	25	19
	Res. of Israel	36	31	31
	No reply	13	15	15
In correspondence with non-Jews in America	Jewish	47	50	47
	American	18	24	17
	Res. of Israel	15	8	14
	No reply	20	18	22
In contact with new immigrants	Jewish	36	17	50
	American	36	57	5
	Res. of Israel	10	12	24
	No reply	18	14	22
When meeting American tourists	Jewish	6	1	17
	American	32	70	22
	Res. of Israel	52	21	50
	No reply	10	8	11
In correspondence with family in America	Jewish	36	32	39
	American	22	28	17
	Res. of Israel	32	28	31
	No reply	10	12	13

21. Alternation of moods during sojourn phases (in per cent; $n = 73$)

How have you felt during the different periods of your stay in Israel?

Period	Very good (1)	Good (2)	Neutral (3)	Bad (4)	Very bad (5)	Median
The first two weeks in Israel	49	31	13	4	3	1.53
The rest of the ulpan period	24	50	14	11	0	2.02
The first two weeks of your university studies	31	37	16	11	4	2.01
The rest of your stay	41	43	13	3	0	1.71

The replies presented diagramatically in the form of a U-curve

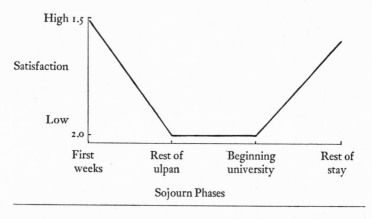

22. Reasons justifying existence of the State of Israel (in per cent; $n = 79$)

Below are five reasons justifying the existence of the State of Israel. Encircle the two reasons which seem to you most important.
The aspirations of Jews through the centuries to return to their homeland

The suffering of the Jews in the Diaspora as a people without
a homeland   44
The recognition by the nations of the world of the idea of a
Jewish State   42
The resettlement of the country in recent times and the War
of Liberation   31
The settlement of the Jewish people in the Land of Israel in
ancient times   26

---

23. Reasons justifying the existence of the State of Israel (in
per cent; $n = 765$) as chosen by Israeli high-school students

---

The suffering of the Jews in the Diaspora as a people without
a homeland   55
The resettlement of the country in recent times and the War
of Liberation   46
The aspirations of the Jews through the centuries to return to
their homeland   37
The settlement of the Jewish people in the Land of Israel in
ancient times   35
The recognition by the nations of the world of the idea of a
Jewish State   27

---

24. Evaluation of antisemitism (in per cent; $n = 73$)

Do you feel that antisemitism is likely to become a serious menace
to the future of American Jewry?
1. I think it is definitely likely to become a serious menace   1
2. I think it is likely to become a serious menace   6
3. I think it may possibly become a serious menace   36
4. I think it will not become a serious menace   44
5. I am sure it will not become a serious menace   13
       Median = 3.68

---

25. Influence of Holocaust, 1966–1967 A.S.P. (in per cent; $n = 83$)

Has the Holocaust (destruction of European Jewry) influenced
your thinking on Jewish life?
                    Yes   84
                    No   15
                    No reply   1

Tables

26. Sources of Israel's attractiveness, 1966–1967 A.S.P. (in per cent; $n = 83$)

What attracts you personally most *about life in Israel? (Choose one of the following.)*

I could feel at home here as a Jew	33
I could live a completely Jewish religious life here	13
I could live here in a kibbutz	0
I could participate in the social ideals of the country	6
I could take part in pioneering activities	7
I could enjoy a more complete Jewish cultural life	15
I like the people	11
Some other factor	13
No reply	2

---

27. Religiosity and intention to settle (medians)

Orthodox	2.37	$(n = 11)$
Nonreligious	2.63	$(n = 24)$
Conservative	3.10	$(n = 24)$
Reform	3.17	$(n = 15)$

1 = yes; 2 = likely; 3 = possibly; 4 = unlikely; 5 = no.

Note: Of the 79 students who answered the first questionnaire, 5 did not indicate with which of the religious subgroups they were affiliated.

---

28. Evaluation by students of desire of religious subgroups to settle, 1966–1967 A.S.P.

Which of the following categories are most likely to have a desire to settle in Israel?

	All respondents ($n = 83$)	Orthodox ($n = 24$)		Conservative ($n = 32$)		Reform ($n = 7$)		Nonreligious ($n = 9$)		Unclassified ($n = 11$)	
	%	%	(n)	%	(n)	%	(n)	%	(n)	%	(n)
1. Orthodox Jews	48	71	(17)	38	(12)	43	(3)	33	(3)	46	(5)
2. Conservative Jews	16	8	(2)	25	(8)	14	(1)	22	(2)	0	(0)
3. Reform Jews	1	0	(0)	0	(0)	0	(0)	0	(0)	9	(1)
4. Nonreligious Jews	8	4	(1)	9	(3)	14	(1)	11	(1)	9	(1)
No reply	27	17	(4)	28	(9)	29	(2)	33	(3)	36	(4)

29. Intention to settle, students at Institute

Do you intend to settle in Israel?

	Chalutzim				Nonchalutzim			
	Before arrival ($n = 27$)		After sojourn ($n = 25$)		Before arrival ($n = 31$)		After sojourn ($n = 29$)	
	%	(n)	%	(n)	%	(n)	%	(n)
1. Yes	100	(27)	88	(22)	0	(0)	45	(13)
2. Undecided, but likely to do so	0		12	(3)	13	(4)	21	(6)
3. Undecided, but may possibly do so	0		0		64	(20)	31	(9)
4. Undecided, but unlikely to do so	0		0		23	(7)	0	(0)
5. No	0		0		0		3	(1)
Median	1.00		1.07		3.07		1.73	

30. Gradual changes in intention to settle, students at Institute ($n = 31$) [a]

	Students whose intention changed			
Extent of change	During first half year in Israel		During second half year in Israel	
	%	(n)	%	(n)
Intention strengthened by two rungs of ladder	14	(4)	7	(2)
Intention strengthened by one rung	45	(14)	36	(11)
Intention unchanged	34	(11)	50	(16)

30. Gradual changes in intention to settle, students at Institute $(n = 31)^a$ *(continued)*

Extent of change	Students whose intention changed	
	During first half year in Israel	During second half year in Israel
Intention weakened	7 (2)	7 (2)

Ladder: 1 = yes; 2 = likely; 3 = possibly; 4 = unlikely; 5 = no.

[a] This table refers only to those students whose intention *could* be strengthened, i.e., who had not already upon arrival in Israel declared the firmest intention ("Yes") to settle in the country.

31. Settlement in Israel as requirement for being "a good Jew" (in per cent)

Is a readiness to "settle in Israel or encourage his children to settle" a requirement for being a "good Jew"?

	A.S.P. students $(n = 73)$	Israeli high-school pupils $(n = 781)$
Essential	2	39
Very desirable	9	26
Desirable	23	16
Irrelevant	65	19
Median	3.74	1.92

1 = essential; 2 = very desirable; 3 = desirable; 4 = irrelevant.

32. Intention to settle, A.S.P. students (in per cent)

Have you ever thought of settling in Israel?

	Before arrival $(n = 79)$	After sojourn $(n = 73)$
1. Yes, I intend to settle	4	11
2. Undecided but likely to do so	9	10
3. Undecided but may possibly do so	46	41
4. Undecided but unlikely to do so	27	23
5. No	14	15
Median	3.30	3.21

33. Gradual changes in intention to settle, A.S.P. students (in per cent; $n = 73$)

Intention strengthened by two rungs	4
Intention strengthened by one rung	28
Intention unchanged	47
Intention weakened by one rung	17
Intention weakened by two rungs	4

34. Feelings of kinship with Jews (in per cent)

Do you regard Jews of all countries as your kith and kin?

	Before arrival ($n = 79$)	After sojourn ($n = 73$)
1. I regard Jews of all countries as my kith and kin	83	73
2. I regard Jews of most countries as my kith and kin	8	9
3. I regard only Jews of some countries as my kith and kin	4	4
4. I regard only American Jews as my kith and kin	0	1
5. I do not regard Jews as my kith and kin	6	13
Median	1.11	1.18

* 35. Similarity among Jews in culture and customs (in per cent)

Are Jews similar to one another in culture and customs?

	Before arrival ($n = 79$)	After sojourn ($n = 73$)
1. Very similar	13	1
2. Similar	59	51
3. Only slightly similar	23	39
4. Not at all similar	5	9
Median	2.13	2.46

$p < .05$

Tables

* 36. Similarity among Jews in characteristics and behavior (in per cent)

Are Jews similar to one another in their characteristics and behavior?

	Before arrival ($n = 79$)	After sojourn ($n = 73$)
1. Very similar	6	1
2. Similar	42	28
3. Only slightly similar	41	52
4. Not at all similar	11	19
Median	2.55	2.90

$p < .01$

* 37. Similarity among Jews in appearance (in per cent)

Are Jews similar to one another in their appearance?

	Before arrival ($n = 79$)	After sojourn ($n = 73$)
1. Very similar	0	0
2. Similar	11	15
3. Only slightly similar	53	24
4. Not at all similar	35	61
Median	3.23	3.68

$p < .01$

38. Comparison of measures of similarity perceived before arrival in Israel (medians; $n = 79$)

Nature of similarity	Among Jews	Between Israelis and American Jews
Culture and customs	2.13	2.82
Characteristics and behavior	2.55	3.18
Appearance	3.23	3.02

1 = very similar; 2 = similar; 3 = only slightly similar; 4 = not at all similar.

39. Similarity between Israelis and American Jews in culture and customs (in per cent)

Do you expect to find (in Questionnaire II—Did you find) Israelis similar to American Jews in their culture and customs?

	Before arrival ($n = 79$)	After sojourn ($n = 73$)
1. Very similar	1	0
2. Similar	32	34
3. Only slightly similar	53	50
4. Not at all similar	14	16
Median	2.82	2.82

40. Similarity between Israelis and American Jews in characteristics and behavior (in per cent)

Do you expect to find (in Questionnaire II—Did you find) Israelis similar to American Jews in their characteristics and behavior?

	Before arrival ($n = 79$)	After sojourn ($n = 73$)
1. Very similar	1	0
2. Similar	11	27
3. Only slightly similar	56	46
4. Not at all similar	32	26
Median	3.18	3.00

* 41. Similarity between Israelis and American Jews in appearance (in per cent)

Do you expect to find (in Questionnaire II—Did you find) Israelis similar to American Jews in their appearance?

	Before arrival ($n = 79$)	After sojourn ($n = 73$)
1. Very similar	1	4
2. Similar	27	37
3. Only slightly similar	42	37
4. Not at all similar	30	22
Median	3.00	2.74

$p < .05$

42. Comparison of measure of similarity perceived before arrival in Israel and that perceived after sojourn (medians)

Nature of similarity	Among Jews		Between Israelis and American Jews	
	Before arrival ($n = 79$)	After sojourn ($n = 73$)	Before arrival ($n = 79$)	After sojourn ($n = 73$)
Culture and customs	2.13	2.46	2.82	2.82
Characteristics and behavior	2.55	2.90	3.18	3.00
Appearance	3.23	3.68	3.02	2.74

1 = very similar; 2 = similar; 3 = only slightly similar; 4 = not at all similar.

43. Reaction to insult of Jewish People (in per cent)

When a British journal insults the Jewish people, do you feel as if it is insulting you?

	Before arrival ($n = 79$)	After sojourn ($n = 73$)
1. Always	39	35
2. Often	52	56
3. Seldom	4	7
4. Never	5	1
Median	1.71	1.76

44. Sense of common fate (in per cent)

Do you feel that your fate and future are bound up with the fate and future of the Jewish people?

	Before arrival ($n = 79$)	After sojourn ($n = 73$)
1. Yes, definitely	47	37
2. To a large extent	29	36
3. To some extent only	22	21
4. No	3	7
Median	1.62	1.88

45. Decline in prestige of American Jewry as it affects Israel (in per cent)

When the prestige of the American Jewish community is lowered, does this affect the State of Israel?

	Before arrival ($n = 79$)	After sojourn ($n = 73$)
1. Almost always	20	14
2. Often	47	58
3. Seldom	22	18
4. Never	11	10
Median	2.14	2.12

46. Decline in prestige of Israel as it affects American Jewry (in per cent)

When the prestige of the State of Israel is lowered, does this affect the American Jewish community?

	Before arrival ($n = 79$)	After sojourn ($n = 73$)
1. Almost always	30	22
2. Often	53	56
3. Seldom	11	18
4. Never	5	4
Median	1.87	2.00

47. Responsibility of Israel to American Jewry (in per cent)

Do you think it is the duty of the State of Israel to help the American Jewish community in time of need?

	Before arrival ($n = 79$)	After sojourn ($n = 73$)
1. Yes, in every case	22	28
2. Yes, but only if the help does not result in a serious detriment to the State of Israel	42	39
3. Yes, but only if the help does not result in any detriment at all to the State of Israel	5	6
4. No	8	11
5. Another response	23	17

Tables

48. Responsibility of American Jewry to help Israel (in per cent)

Do you think it is the duty of the American Jewish community to help the State of Israel in time of need?

	Before arrival (n = 79)	After sojourn (n = 73)
1. Yes, in every case	56	58
2. Yes, but only if the help does not result in a serious detriment to the American Jewish community	27	26
3. Yes, but only if the help does not result in any detriment at all to the American Jewish community	3	3
4. No	0	3
5. Another response	16	11

Semantic Differential: Instructions, Tables 49–53

On the following pages you will find groups to be judged by you. There follows a series of scales and you are asked to rate the group in question on each of these scales in order.

If you feel that the group at the top of the page is very closely related to one end of the scale, you should place your checkmark as follows:

fair : x : : : : : : unfair
or
fair : : : : : : : x : unfair

If you feel that the group is quite closely related *to one or the other end of the scale* (but not extremely), *you should place your checkmark as follows:*

fair : : x : : : : : unfair
or
fair : : : : : : x : unfair

If the groups seems only slightly related *to one side as opposed to the other side, then you should check as follows:*

fair : : : x : : : : unfair
or
fair : : : : : x : : unfair

The direction toward which you check, of course, depends upon which of the two ends of the scale seems most characteristic of the thing you're judging.

49. Ratings on Semantic Differential before arrival in Israel (mean values; $n = 79$)

Adjective pairs	Concepts				
	American Jew	American non-Jew	Israeli	Myself as I am	Myself as I would like to be
Unsociable–sociable [a]	5.80	5.24	5.11	5.54	6.32
Lazy–industrious	6.07	4.98	6.14	5.13	6.52
Unpleasant–pleasant	5.34	5.12	4.90	5.65	6.50
Weak–strong	4.51	4.42	5.80	4.70	6.34
Man of words–man of deeds	4.24	4.15	5.68	4.61	6
Conservative–progressive	5.51	3.44	5.66	5.56	6.15
Dishonest–honest	4.79	4.55	5.04	6.15	6.58
Constrained–free	4.08	4.24	5.85	5.06	6.42
Stupid–clever	5.65	4.28	5.70	5.47	6.64
Ugly–beautiful	4.34	4.23	4.76	4.68	6.05
Cold–warm	5.42	4.26	4.94	5.61	6.60
Intolerant–tolerant	5.06	3.71	3.93	6.03	6.70
Inhospitable–hospitable	5.51	5.41	5.52	6.07	6.58
Discourteous–courteous	4.80	4.86	3.96	5.85	6.26
Lacking self-respect–self-respecting	5.18	5.04	6.01	5.70	6.71
Ashamed of his Americanism–proud of his Americanism	5.68	6.06	—	5.63	6.05
Irreligious–religious	3.39	4.39	3.11	4.50	5.06
Ashamed of his Jewishness–proud of his Jewishness	4.52	—	5.90	6.44	6.58
Lacking roots in Jewishness–with roots in Jewishness	4.34	—	5.68	5.86	6.47
Materialistic–idealistic	2.75	2.82	4.37	4.93	5.23
Ashamed of being an Israeli–proud of being an Israeli	—	—	6.62	—	—

[a] Adjective pairs have been rearranged so that the adjective with the unfavorable connotation appears on the left and the adjective with the favorable connotation on the right. The higher the mean, the greater the measure of favorableness.

50. Mean value of concepts on Semantic Differential before arrival in Israel and toward the end of the sojourn

Concepts	Before ($n = 79$)	After ($n = 73$)
American non-Jew	4.53	—
American Jew	5.09	5.08
Israeli	5.27	4.74
Myself as I am	5.46	5.37
Myself as I would like to be	6.71	—

51. Ratings on Semantic Differential toward the end of the sojourn (mean values; $n = 73$)

Adjective pairs	American Jew	Myself as I am	Israeli
Unsociable–sociable	5.85 (+0.05) [a]	5.31 (−0.23)	4.34 (−0.77)
Lazy–industrious	5.94 (−0.13)	4.70 (−0.47)	5.61 (−0.53)
Unpleasant–pleasant	5.31 (−0.03)	5.61 (−0.04)	4.59 (−0.31)
Weak–strong	4.51 (0.00)	4.66 (−0.04)	5.58 (−0.22)
Man of words–man of deeds	4.44 (+0.20)	4.52 (−0.09)	5.24 (−0.44)
Conservative–progressive	5.41 (−0.10)	5.41 (−0.15)	3.82 (−1.84)
Dishonest–honest	5.06 (+0.27)	6.34 (+0.19)	4.75 (−0.39)
Constrained–free	4.49 (+0.41)	5.10 (+0.04)	5.24 (−0.61)
Stupid–clever	5.37 (−0.28)	5.35 (+0.23)	5.07 (−0.63)
Ugly–beautiful	4.39 (+0.05)	4.68 (0.00)	4.38 (−0.38)
Cold–warm	5.10 (−0.32)	5.48 (−0.20)	4.46 (−0.48)
Intolerant–tolerant	5.03 (−0.03)	5.93 (−0.10)	3.55 (−0.38)
Inhospitable–hospitable	5.13 (−0.38)	5.89 (−0.18)	5.79 (+0.27)
Discourteous–courteous	5.13 (+0.33)	5.93 (+0.08)	2.77 (−1.19)
Lacking self-respect–self-respecting	5.13 (−0.05)	5.66 (−0.04)	5.97 (−0.04)
Ashamed of his Americanism–proud of his Americanism	5.72 (+0.04)	5.73 (+0.10)	——
Irreligious–religious	3.87 (+0.48)	4.72 (+0.13)	2.90 (−0.21)
Ashamed of his Jewishness–proud of his Jewishness	4.63 (+0.11)	6.32 (−0.12)	5.56 (−0.34)
Lacking roots in Jewishness–with roots in Jewishness	4.48 (+0.14)	6.08 (+0.22)	5.04 (−0.64)

Adjective pairs	American Jew	Myself as I am	Israeli
Materialistic–idealistic	3.20 (+0.45)	4.77 (−0.16)	3.32 (−1.05)
Ashamed of being an Israeli–proud of being an Israeli	——	——	6.66 (+0.04)

^a The figure in parentheses indicates the difference between the ratings on the Semantic Differential administered before arrival in Israel and toward the end of the sojourn. A plus sign indicates change in a favorable direction, a minus sign in an unfavorable one.

52. Semantic Differential: ratings of concept "Israeli" on social contact variables (mean values)

Adjective pairs	Before arrival ($n = 79$)	After sojourn ($n = 73$)
Inhospitable–hospitable	5.52	5.79
Discourteous–courteous	3.96	2.77
Cold–warm	4.94	4.46
Unsociable–sociable	5.11	4.34

53. Differences between ratings of "Israeli" and "Myself as I am" (mean values)

Adjective pairs	Before arrival ($n = 79$)	After sojourn ($n = 73$)
Unsociable–sociable	0.43 [a]	0.97 [a]
Lazy–industrious	1.01	0.91
Unpleasant–pleasant	0.75 [a]	1.02 [a]
Weak–strong	1.10	0.92
Man of words–man of deeds	1.07	0.62
Conservative–progressive	0.10	1.59 [a]
Dishonest–honest	1.11 [a]	1.59 [a]
Constrained–free	0.79	0.14
Stupid–clever	0.28	0.28 [a]
Ugly–beautiful	0.08	0.30 [a]
Cold–warm	0.75 [a]	1.02 [a]
Intolerant–tolerant	2.10 [a]	2.38 [a]
Inhospitable–hospitable	0.55 [a]	0.10 [a]
Discourteous–courteous	1.89 [a]	3.16 [a]
Lacking self-respect–self-respecting	0.31	0.31

53. Differences between ratings of "Israeli" and "Myself as I am" (mean values) (*continued*)

Adjective pairs	Before arrival (n = 79)	After sojourn (n = 73)
Irreligious–religious	1.48 [a]	1.80 [a]
Ashamed of his Jewishness–proud of his Jewishness	0.55 [a]	0.76 [a]
Lacking roots in Jewishness–with roots	0.18 [a]	1.04 [a]
Materialistic–idealistic	0.56 [a]	1.45 [a]

[a] An "a" after the rating signifies that "myself" has the higher score. Where there is no "a," "Israeli" has the higher score.

54. Impression of Israel and Israelis (in per cent)

Impression	Israel		Israelis	
	Before arrival (n = 79)	After sojourn (n = 73)	Before arrival (n = 79)	After sojourn (n = 73)
1. Very favorable	33	33	14	7
2. Favorable	65	64	71	71
3. Unfavorable	3	3	14	21
4. Very unfavorable	0	0	0	0
Median	1.77	1.77	2.00	2.11

55. Courses of action open to American Jewry (in per cent)

The following are some courses of action which are open to the American Jewish community; choose the three which you consider most important; write the number 1 next to the course of action which you regard as most important, 2 beside that which is next in your order of preference, and 3 beside the third preference.

	Before arrival (n = 79)	After sojourn (n = 73)
Improve relations between Jews and non-Jews	42	29
Encourage the Jewish education of youth	82	85

	Before arrival ($n = 79$)	After sojourn ($n = 73$)
Spread a knowledge of Hebrew among the Jewish community	19	15
Fight antisemitism	10	10
Encourage American Jewish immigration to Israel	9	11
Develop the Zionist movement	7	8
Stimulate the contribution of Jews to the United States	6	8
Strengthen democratic processes in the United States	29	27
Persuade the American people to extend political and moral support to Israel	24	23
Encourage the material support of American Jewry for Israel	18	18
Strengthen the local Jewish community organization	22	32
Strengthen Jewish religious practices	26	30

In the Table the three choices are given equal weight.

56. Intention to be active in Jewish affairs in America (in per cent; $n = 73$)

Do you think that on your return to America you are likely to be more active or less active in Jewish affairs?

More active	51
As active as before	30
Less active	9
As inactive as before	10

57. Memory of the Holocaust, 1966–1967 A.S.P. ($n = 33$)

Were you at any time during these weeks reminded of the Holocaust (destruction of European Jewry)?

	%	(n)
Yes	87	(29)
No	12	(4)

58. Comparison of feelings before and after Six Day War, 1966–1967 A.S.P. ($n = 33$)

How do you feel today in the present situation, compared to your feelings before the War? More American, less American, as American as before? More Israeli, less Israeli, as Israeli as before? More Jewish, less Jewish, as Jewish as before?

	Israeli		Jewish		American	
	%	(n)	%	(n)	%	(n)
Feel more	66	(22)	54	(18)	3	(1)
Feel as	30	(10)	45	(15)	57	(19)
Feel less	3	(1)	0	(0)	39	(13)

59. Salience of Americanism after return to the United States ($n = 29$)

A person with a strong feeling of being American		A person with no feeling of being American
	: 7 : 6 : 5 : 4 : 3 : 2 : 1 :	
During sojourn in Israel	: 10 : 45 : 7 : 17 : 3 : 17 : 0 :	Median = 5.61
After a year in U.S.	: 7 : 31 : 14 : 14 : 17 : 17 : 0 :	Median = 4.62

$p < 0.01$

* 60. Salience of Jewishness after return to the United States ($n = 29$)

A person with a strong feeling of being Jewish		A person with no feeling of being Jewish
	: 7 : 6 : 5 : 4 : 3 : 2 : 1 :	
During sojourn in Israel	: 35 : 41 : 7 : 14 : 0 : 3 : 0 :	Median = 6.11
After a year in U.S.	: 52 : 31 : 10 : 3 : 3 : 0 : 0 :	Median = 6.53

$p < 0.05$

* 61. Attitude toward Israel after a year in the United States

What is the impression you now have about Israel?

	During sojourn		After year in U.S.	
	%	(n = 27)	%	(n = 29)
1. Very favorable	24	(7)	59	(17)
2. Favorable	72	(19)	38	(11)
3. Unfavorable	3	(1)	3	(1)
4. Very unfavorable	0	(0)	0	(0)
Median	1.86		1.35	

$p < 0.01$

* 62. Attitude toward Israelis after a year in the United States

What is the impression you now have about Israelis?

	During sojourn		After year in U.S.	
	%	(n = 27)	%	(n = 29)
1. Very favorable	7	(2)	34	(10)
2. Favorable	67	(18)	59	(17)
3. Unfavorable	26	(7)	7	(2)
4. Very unfavorable	0	(0)	0	(0)
Median	2.10		1.76	

$p < 0.005$

63. Sensitivity to insult of Israel after a year in the United States (in per cent; $n = 29$)

When a British journal insults Israel, do you feel as if it is insulting you?

	During sojourn		After year in U.S.	
	%	(n)	%	(n)
1. Always	7	(2)	17	(5)
2. Often	69	(20)	59	(17)
3. Seldom	10	(3)	17	(5)
4. Never	14	(4)	7	(2)
Median	2.12		2.06	

Tables

64. Sensitivity to praise of Israel after a year in the United States (in per cent; $n = 29$)

When a British journal praises Israel, do you feel as if it is praising you?

	During sojourn		After year in U.S.	
	%	(n)	%	(n)
1. Always	7	(2)	17	(5)
2. Often	55	(16)	59	(17)
3. Seldom	17	(5)	10	(3)
4. Never	21	(6)	14	(4)
Median	2.28		2.06	

65. Intention to settle after a year in the United States ($n = 29$)

How do you feel now about settling in Israel?

	During sojourn		After year in U.S.	
	%	(n)	%	(n)
1. Yes, I intend to settle	17	(5)	24	(7)
2. Undecided but likely to do so	7	(2)	10	(3)
3. Undecided but may possibly do so	41	(12)	41	(12)
4. Undecided but unlikely to do so	24	(7)	10	(3)
5. No	10	(3)	14	(4)
Median	3.11		2.87	

66. Gradual change in intention to settle after return to the United States, 1965–1966 A.S.P.

Extent of change	%	(n)
Intention strengthened by two rungs	7	(2)
Intention strengthened by one rung	28	(8)
Intention unchanged	52	(15)
Intention weakened by one rung	10	(3)
Intention weakened by two rungs	3	(1)
	100	(29)

67. Evaluation of antisemitism by American students in a psychology class at the Hebrew University in 1969 ($n = 36$), and by A.S.P. group in 1965 ($n = 73$) (in per cent)

Do you feel that antisemitism is likely to become a serious menace to the future of American Jewry?

	1969	1965
1. I think it is definitely likely to become a serious menace	6	1
2. I think it is likely to become a serious menace	22	6
3. I think it may possibly become a serious menace	42	36
4. I think it will not become a serious menace	28	44
5. I am sure it will not become a serious menace	3	13
Median	3.03	3.68

68. Consciousness of Holocaust (on part of American students in a psychology class at the Hebrew University in 1969)

Jews—wherever they be and even if they or their parents were never in Europe—should look upon themselves as if they are survivors of the Holocaust (the destruction of six million Jews in Europe).

	%	($n = 37$)
1. Agree	73	(27)
2. Disagree	27	(10)

Glossary of Hebrew Terms

aliyah—(literally "ascent") immigration to Israel

chag (pl. chagim)—festival

chalutz (pl. chalutzim)—pioneer

chofesh—freedom; vacation

chutz la'aretz—countries outside of Israel; the Diaspora

davka—despite it all

erev—on the eve

galuth—the Exile

kibbutz (pl. kibbutzim)—collective settlement

kibbutznik—colloquial reference to member of a kibbutz

kipah—skull-cap worn by Orthodox Jews

machon—institute (The institute referred to here is the Institute for Overseas Youth Leaders in Jerusalem.)

machonik—colloquial reference to member of the institute

madrich (pl. madrichim)—guide, counselor

mechitza—partition in Orthodox synagogues between seating arrangements for men and women

milu'im—reservists in the Israel Defense Forces

mitzvah (pl. mitzvoth)—a religious obligation

moshav (pl. moshavim)—smallholders' settlement

sabra (from tzabar; literally a cactus)—a native-born Israeli

shabat—Sabbath

sherut la'am—"service to the people," and *sh'nat sherut*, "a year of service," work programs for visiting youth sponsored by the Jewish Agency

succoth—booths erected on *Succoth*, festival of the Tabernacles

Glossary

tiyul (pl. tiyulim)—excursion into the country, hike

ulpan—residential seminar for the intensive study of Hebrew

Yahadut—Judaism

Yeshiva—religious academy; a religion-oriented Jewish day school

Yom Kippur—Day of Atonement

Bibliography

Adams, W., ed. *The Brain Drain.* New York: Macmillan, 1968.

Annals of the American Academy of Political and Social Science. No. 295, 1954.

Barker, R. G., T. Dembo, and K. Lewin. "Adjustment to Physical Handicap and Illness," *Social Science Research Council Bulletin,* No. 55 (1953).

——, T. Dembo, and K. Lewin. *Frustration and Regression: An Experiment with Young Children,* Studies in Topological and Vector Psychology, II. Iowa City: University of Iowa Press, 1941.

Beals, R. L., and N. D. Humphrey. *No Frontier to Learning: The Mexican Student in the United States.* Minneapolis: University of Minnesota Press, 1957.

Bennett, J. W., H. Passin, and R. K. McKnight. *In Search of Identity: The Japanese Overseas Scholar in America and Japan.* Minneapolis: University of Minnesota Press, 1958.

Berkowitz, L., and L. R. Daniels. "Affecting the Salience of the Social Responsibility Norm: Effects of Past Help on the Response to Dependency Relationships," *Journal of Abnormal and Social Psychology,* LXVIII (1964), 275–281.

Brown, L. B. "English Migrants to New Zealand: The Decision to Move," *Human Relations,* XIII (1960), 167–174.

Bruner, J. S., and H. V. Perlmutter. "Compatriot and Foreigner: A Study of Impression Formation in Three Countries," *Journal of Abnormal and Social Psychology,* LV (1957), 253–260.

Bibliography

Cartwright, D. R. "Achieving Change in People," *Human Relations*, IV (1951), 381–392.

Charters, W. W., and T. M. Newcomb. "Some Attitudinal Effects of Experimentally Increased Salience of a Membership Group," *Readings in Social Psychology*, ed. E. E. Maccoby, T. M. Newcomb, and E. L. Hartley. 3d ed. New York: Holt, 1958, pp. 276–281.

Chein, I. "The Problem of Jewish Identification," *Jewish Social Studies*, XVII (1955), 219–222.

——, S. W. Cook, and J. Harding. "The Field of Action Research," *American Psychologist*, III (1948), 43–50.

Child, I. L. *Italian or American? The Second Generation in Conflict*. New Haven: Yale University Press, 1943.

Coelho, G. V. *Changing Images of America: A Study of Indian Students' Perceptions*. Glencoe, Ill.: Free Press, 1958.

Conster, H. L. "Criteria for Measures of Association," *American Sociological Review*, XXX (1965), 341–352.

Cook, S. W., and C. Selltiz. "Some Factors Which Influence the Attitudinal Outcomes of Personal Contact," *International Social Science Bulletin*, VII (1955), 51–58.

Du Bois, C. *Foreign Students and Higher Education in the United States*. Washington: American Council on Education, 1956.

Eisenstadt, S. N. *The Absorption of Immigrants*. London: Routledge, 1954.

Elliot, A. J. A. "The Evaluation of International Education: An Administrative Approach," *Social Sciences Information*, IV (1965), 61–78.

——. "Foreign Students in Perspective," *Social Sciences Information*, VI (1967), 189–202.

Erikson, E. H. *Childhood and Society*. New York: Norton, 1950.

——. "Ego Identity and the Psychosocial Moratorium," *New Perspectives for Research on Juvenile Delinquency*, ed. H. L. Witner and R. Kotinsky. Washington, D.C.: U.S. Govt. Printing Office, 1955, pp. 1–23.

Bibliography

Festinger, L. *A Theory of Cognitive Dissonance.* Evanston, Ill.: Row, Peterson, 1957.

Frank, L. K. "Time Perspectives," *Journal of Social Philosophy,* IV (1939), 293–312.

French, J. R. P., and R. B. Zajonc. "An Experimental Study of Cross-Cultural Norm Conflict," *Journal of Abnormal and Social Psychology,* LIV (1957), 218–224.

Friedmann, G. *The End of the Jewish People?* New York: Doubleday, 1967.

Fuchs, L. *The Political Behavior of American Jews.* Glencoe, Ill.: Free Press, 1956.

Ginzberg, E. *Occupational Choice.* New York: Columbia University Press, 1951.

Goffman, E. *Stigma: Notes on the Management of Spoiled Identity.* Englewood Cliffs, New Jersey: Prentice-Hall, 1963.

Gullahorn, J. T., and J. E. Gullahorn. "An Extension of the U-Curve Hypothesis," *Journal of Social Issues,* XIX (1963), 33–47.

Herman, S. N. "Explorations in the Social Psychology of Language Choice," *Human Relations,* XIV (1961), 149–164.

———. *Israelis and Jews: A Study in the Continuity of an Identity.* New York: Random House, forthcoming.

———. "Mesilot la Ziyonut hehaluzit" ["Pathways to Chalutzic Zionism"], *Ha-Ziyonut be-Sha'a zu* ["*Zionism in the Contemporary Period*], ed. G. Hanoch. Jerusalem: Zionist Organization, 1951, pp. 131–137.

———, and E. O. Schild. "Ethnic Role Conflict in a Cross-Cultural Situation," *Human Relations,* XIII (1960), 215–228.

———, Y. Peres, and E. Yuchtman. "Reactions to the Eichmann Trial in Israel: A Study in High Involvement," *Scripta Hierosolymitana,* XIV (The Hebrew University, Jerusalem: Magnes Press, 1965), 98–118.

Hofman, J. E., and I. Zak. "Interpersonal Contact and Attitude Change in a Cross-Cultural Situation," *Journal of Social Psychology,* LXXVIII (1969), 165–171.

Institute of International Education. *Annual Report.* New York, 1965.

——. *Open Doors.* New York, 1968.

International Social Science Bulletin. No. 7, 1955.

Jacobson, E. "Sojourn Research: A Definition of the Field," *Journal of Social Issues,* XIX (1963), 123–129.

Jahoda, M. "Conformity and Independence: A Psychological Analysis," *Human Relations,* XII (1960), 99–119.

Journal of Social Issues. No. 1, 1956.

——. No. 1, 1962.

——. No. 3, 1963.

Kastenbaum, R. "The Structure and Function of Time Perspective," *Journal of Psychological Researches,* VIII (1964), 1–11.

Kelley, H. H. "Salience of Membership and Resistance to Change of Group-Anchored Attitudes," *Human Relations,* VIII (1955), 275–289.

Kelman, H., ed. *International Behavior: A Social Psychological Analysis.* New York: Holt, Rinehart and Winston, 1965.

Killian, L. M. "The Significance of Multiple-Group Membership in Disaster," *American Journal of Sociology,* LVII (1952), 309–314.

Klineberg, O. "The Multi-National Society: Some Research Problems," *Social Sciences Information,* VI (1967), 81–99.

——. "Research in the Field of International Exchanges in Education, Science and Culture," *Social Sciences Information,* IV (1965), 97–138.

Lambert, R. D., and M. Bressler. *Indian Students on an American Campus.* Minneapolis: University of Minnesota Press, 1956.

——, and M. Bressler. "The Sensitive-area Complex: A Contribution to the Theory of Guided Culture Contact," *American Journal of Sociology,* LX (1955), 583–592.

Lambert, W. E., E. Libman, and E. G. Poser. "The Effect of

Increased Salience of a Membership Group on Pain Tolerance," *Journal of Personality*, XXVIII (1960), 350–357.

Lesser, S. O., and H. W. Peter. "Training Foreign Nationals in the United States," *Some Applications of Behavioral Research*, ed. R. Likert and S. P. Hayes. UNESCO, 1957, pp. 160–206.

Lewin, K. *Resolving Social Conflicts*, ed. G. W. Lewin. New York: Harper, 1948.

——. *Field Theory in Social Science*, ed. D. Cartwright. New York: Harper, 1951.

——. "Intention, Will and Need," *Organization and Pathology of Thought*, ed. D. Rapaport. New York: Columbia University Press, 1951.

Lysgaard, S. "Adjustment in a Foreign Society: Norwegian Fulbright Grantees Visiting the United States," *International Social Science Bulletin*, VII (1955), 45–51.

Marrow, A. J., and J. R. P. French, Jr. "Changing a Stereotype in Industry," *Journal of Social Issues*, I (1945), 33–37.

Merton, R. K. *Social Theory and Social Structure*. Glencoe, Ill.: Free Press, 1957.

——, G. G. Reader, and P. L. Kendall. *The Student Physician: Introductory Studies in the Sociology of Medical Education*. Cambridge, Mass.: Harvard University Press, 1957.

Mills, C. Wright, C. Senior, and R. K. Goldsen. *The Puerto Rican Journey*. New York: Harper, 1950.

Morris, R. T. *The Two-Way Mirror: National Status in Foreign Students' Adjustment*. Minneapolis: University of Minnesota Press, 1960.

Newcomb, T. M., and E. K. Wilson, eds. *College Peer Groups*. Chicago: Aldine, 1966.

Osgood, C. E., G. J. Suci, and P. H. Tannenbaum. *The Measurement of Meaning*. Urbana: University of Illinois Press, 1957.

Parsons, T. "The Position of Identity in the General Theory

of Action," *The Self in Social Interaction,* ed. Gordon and K. J. Gergen. Vol. I. New York: Wiley, 1968, pp. 11–23.

PEP (Political and Economic Planning). *Colonial Students in Britain.* London, 1955.

Pool, I. de Sola. "Effects of Cross-National Contact on National and International Images," *International Behavior: A Social Psychological Analysis,* ed. H. Kelman. New York: Holt, Rinehart and Winston, 1965.

Rossi, P. H. "Why Families Move," *The Language of Social Research,* ed. P. F. Lazarsfeld and M. Rosenberg. Glencoe, Ill.: Free Press, 1955, pp. 457–468.

Schachter, S. *The Psychology of Affiliation.* Stanford, Calif.: Stanford University Press, 1959.

Schuetz, A. "The Stranger: An Essay in Social Psychology," *American Journal of Sociology,* XLIX (1944), 499–507.

Scott, F. D. *The American Experience of Swedish Students.* Minneapolis: University of Minnesota Press, 1956.

Selltiz, C., S. W. Cook, J. R. Christ, and J. Havel. *Attitudes and Social Relations of Foreign Students in the United States.* Minneapolis: University of Minnesota Press, 1963.

Sewell, W., and O. Davidsen. *Scandinavian Students on an American Campus.* Minneapolis: University of Minnesota Press, 1961.

Shuval, J. T. *Immigrants on the Threshold.* New York: Atherton Press, 1963.

Sklare, M., and J. Greenblum. *Jewish Identity on the Suburban Frontier: A Study of Group Survival in the Open Society.* The Lakeville Studies, vol. I. New York: Basic Books, 1967.

Smith, M. B., J. T. Fawcett, R. Ezekiel, and S. Roth. "A Factorial Study of Morale among Peace Corps Teachers in Ghana," *Journal of Social Issues,* XIX (1963), 10–32.

Stein, M. I. *Volunteers for Peace: The First Group of Peace Corps Volunteers in a Rural Community Development*

Program in Colombia, South America. New York: Wiley, 1965.

Stember, C. H., et al. *Jews in the Mind of America.* New York: Basic Books, 1966.

Stouffer, S. A. "An Analysis of Conflicting Social Norms," *American Sociological Review,* XIV (1949), 707–717.

UNESCO. *Study Abroad,* XVI (Paris, 1966), and XVII (1968).

Useem, J., and R. Useem. *The Western-Educated in India: A Study of His Social Roles and Influence.* New York: Dryden Press, 1955.

Wagley, C., and M. Harris. *Minorities in the New World.* New York: Columbia University Press, 1958.

Watson, J., and R. Lippitt. *Learning across Cultures: A Study of Germans Visiting America.* Research Center for Group Dynamics Series, Publication 4. Ann Arbor: University of Michigan, 1955.

White, R. W. *Lives in Progress.* New York: Dryden Press, 1952.

Williams, R. M., Jr. *Strangers Next Door: Ethnic Relations in American Communities.* Englewood Cliffs, New Jersey: Prentice-Hall, 1964.

Wolff, K. H., ed. *The Sociology of Georg Simmel.* Glencoe, Ill.: Free Press, 1950.

Yarrow, M. R. "Personality Development and Minority Group Membership," *The Jews: Social Patterns of an American Group,* ed. M. Sklare. Glencoe, Ill.: Free Press, 1957, pp. 451–474.

Zajonc, R. B. "Aggressive Attitudes of the Stranger as a Function of Conformity Pressures," *Human Relations,* V (1952), 205–216.

Index

Index

Students, American Jewish (*cont.*)
  and Israeli religious practices, 49-51, 60, 87-88, 107, 131-132, 135
  and kibbutzim, *see* Kibbutzim
  on kinship of Jews, 106-110, 134, 137, 139
  knowledge of Hebrew, 51, 60, 127, 132-133
  learning, *see* Learning in host society
  morale of, 84
  and multiple group references, 7-8
  in overlapping situations, 36, 69-77
  participation in Israeli activities, 169
  perspective on United States, *see* United States
  reactions to views of Israelis, 67-68, 72
  relationships with Israelis, 48-51, 55-68, 113, 127-128, 133, 140-142
  religious views, 95-96
  roles played by, 69, 74-77
  and Six Day War, *see* Six Day War
  as stranger group, 11-13, 51-54, 55, 64-66, 67, 98, 106, 136, 168-169
  time perspective of, 78-88, 91-92, 138-139
  views on Israel and Israelis, 66, 78, 86, 87-88, 94-95, 104, 106, 107-108, 110-116, 128, 131-132, 133-135, 141-142; *see also* Students, American Jewish, views after return
Students, American Jewish, views after return, 144-159
  on America vs. Israel, 147-148, 149, 156-157
  on American culture, 145-146
  on American Jewry, 147-148, 149
  on antisemitism, 145, 146
  on immigration to Israel, 155-158
  on influence of stay in Israel, 145
  on Israel and Israelis, 150, 152-155
  on Jewish identity, 144, 149, 169-170
  on membership in minority group, 144, 146
  on relationship to non-Jews, 150-151
  on Six Day War, 158-159
Subidentities, 35-38, 42-43

United States:
  defended by American students in Israel, 71
  return to, 82-83
  ties of American students in Israel with, 89, 90
  views of American students in Israel on, 71, 73, 91-94, 104, 121, 145-146

Valence, 16-18
  of activities in host society, 104-105
  defined, 17
  of roles played by American students in Israel, 74
  of students' American identity, 65-66, 73
  of students' Jewish identity, 73

Zionism:
  influence on American students, 31, 86, 97, 126
  World Zionist Organization, 24-25

Temple Israel
Minneapolis, Minnesota

IN MEMORY OF
SYLVIA ROSTON
FROM
J. D. ROSTON